The Illustrated History *of*
GUNS

The Illustrated History *of*
GUNS

From First Firearms to Semiautomatic Weapons

Chuck Wills
In Association with the Berman Museum of World History
Foreword by Robert A. Sadowski

Skyhorse Publishing

www.skyhorsepublishing.com

10 9 8 7 6 5

Library of Congress Cataloging-in-Publication Data is available on file.

Cover design by Brian Peterson

Print ISBN: 978-1-5107-2074-9
Ebook ISBN: 978-1-5107-1619-3

Printed in China

"The greatest joy a man can know is to conquer his enemies and drive them before him. To ride their horses and take away their possessions. To see the faces of those who were dear to them bedewed with tears, and to clasp their wives and daughters in his arms."
—Genghis Khan

"The root of the evil is not the construction of new, more dreadful weapons. It is the spirit of conquest."
—Ludwig von Mises

"Political power grows out of the barrel of a gun."
—Mao Zedong

Browning High-Powered Pistol

Coehorn Mortar

CONTENTS

Foreword
by Robert A. Sadowski

Try to imagine what life was like before ATM cards, iPads, a GPS, or smartphones. Now imagine what it was like before AR-15 carbines, 1911 pistols, Remington 870 shotguns, or Ruger 10/22 rifles. Technology is constantly evolving, and that is certainly true with respect to firearms.

I'm old enough to remember rotary-dial telephones, the predecessors to push-button analog phones and our current mobile smartphones. I am also old enough to remember when primitive weapon hunting laws were passed and we all scrambled to figure out how to load a percussion rifle with loose powder, a patch, cap, and lead ball. For some it was quite a learning curve. Even modern primitive hunting firearms have evolved and are manufactured with stainless steel so they resist corrosion and polymer stocks. They also use 209 shotgun primers in lieu of precision caps, pellets in place of loose powder, and plastic sabots instead of cloth patches. This is just a snapshot in time of firearm advancements in the last few decades; if we go back to the beginning, you can get a good idea of how weapons have been refined over centuries.

Whether to feed or to protect, there are milestones in the evolution of firearms. Perhaps the most revolutionary was the evolution of the lock. The lock—matchlock, wheellock, flintlock, and eventually percussion lock—was the mechanism that transformed black powder into a combustible gas that explosively pushed a projectile down a tube. Centuries would pass as the lock mechanisms evolved. By the time the flintlock was designed, the firearm—back then a musket or rifle—was state-of-the-art weaponry. The Brown Bess musket is a good example of a milestone in firearm development. The Brown Bess is the nickname given to the British Army smoothbore musket in the eighteenth century. These ten-pound muskets were over fifty-eight inches long and fired a .75 caliber lead ball. Effective range was about fifty to one hundred yards, and depending on how dexterous you were, you could fire three to four rounds per minute. During the American Revolution, Minute Men armed with Brown Bess muskets and whatever other rifles and muskets that were available

Liliput Pistol

Luger with Drum Magazine

fought the British. It is not clear whether the "shot heard round the world," fired in 1775 and starting the American Revolution, was from a Brown Bess, but I am sure one (or several) were present that day at the North Bridge in Concord, Massachusetts. Hunting and warfare dramatically evolved when reliable firearms were designed. The Napoleonic Wars from 1803 to 1825 saw the use of muskets by armies all across Europe and into Asia.

The problem with the first single-shot firearms was their capacity, or lack thereof. Reloading could be time-consuming, especially if an angry grizzly bear were galloping toward you or you were confronted with an enemy swinging an axe or broadsword. Later, firearms were built into axes and other edged weapons. Bayonets, for example, were invented to avoid the reloading problem. After the rifle's one shot was fired, the bayonet allowed the user to continue fighting without the need to reload. The trick was to figure out a way to fire multiple times without the need to reload. Under optimal conditions, a user could reload a musket two to three rounds per minute.

Odd-looking weapons with multiple barrels were designed, but they were awkward and there still was the issue of fast reloading. It was Samuel Colt who designed the first revolver, which used a cylinder with multiple chambers that rotated behind a barrel and allowed the user to fire multiple times without reloading. The Colt Paterson revolver, the first reliable repeating handgun, was the next dramatic development. It was especially decisive in the Battle of Bandera Pass in 1841, where fifty Texas Rangers had ten shots at their disposal. They each carried a pair of five-shot Paterson revolvers that day when they encountered a large band of Comanches. The legend goes that the fifty Texas Rangers held their ground against hundreds of Comanches due to the Rangers' overwhelming firepower of the Paterson revolver. Five shots could be fired as fast as the revolver could be cocked and the trigger pulled.

The next event in the evolution of firearms is the development of the metallic cartridge. The Paterson and other revolvers that followed still required powder and ball to reload. The metallic cartridge used a metallic case filled with powder and a bullet seated in the open end. On the closed end of the case was primer used to ignite the powder and fire the bullet.

The American Civil War, which started in 1861 and ended in 1865, really saw the clash between Napoleonic warfare tactics and more modern weaponry. Napoleon's tactics had opposing armies face each other and slowly walk toward the enemy. Artillery and the use of rifles in the Civil War quickly proved technology in weapons was outpacing military tactics. Perhaps the Henry rife is a good milestone for this era. The Henry used by Union troops toward the end of the war featured metallic cartridges. The saying among Confederate troops was the Henry was "a rifle that you could load on Sunday and shoot all week long."

Metallic cartridges evolved in the mid-nineteenth century, and by the turn of the twentieth century they were the preferred technology. Firearms development occurred rapidly at this point in history.

There are numerous milestones with the development of the metallic cartridge, but one of the most significant is the semiautomatic mechanism. Semiautomatic rifles and pistols allowed users to fire the weapon with each press of the trigger. Prior to semiautomatic weapons, a user manually reloaded the weapon by either working a lever or a bolt and inserting new cartridges one at a time or chambering one from a magazine that held numerous cartridges. The rate of fire from a semiautomatic handgun or rifle was far superior to anything that came before.

Not long after that, fully-automatic weapons were designed. Sir Hiram Maxim invented the machine gun in 1885; it could fire an astounding six hundred rounds per minute. During World War I, the machine gun was employed with devastating results. Nearly an entire generation of young men were killed on both sides due to the use of the machine gun, and it was deadly in nineteenth century–style warfare, in which opposing armies marched toward each other in battle. Bullets raced and bodies fell.

Spanish Cannon

Within The Illustrated History of Guns are the stories and milestones of firearm development from early single-shot smoothbores to machine guns. The stories of the men who invented them and those who used them in battle. It is fascinating to find out how the firearm evolved over the centuries and how they brought us to where we are today.

Robert A. Sadowski
Hampstead, North Carolina
November 29, 2016

Apache

PREFACE

From the first rock held with intention in the hands of Paleolithic man all the way through to the twenty-first century assault rifle, weapons have been an integral component in human history. Early weapons, however, from that Paleolithic "inventor" through the first 1200 years AD, were effective primarily in hand-to-hand combat, save for the use of bows and arrows and catapults of various designs. The invention of gunpowder brought radical change in weaponry and warfare. The first documented battlefield use of gunpowder artillery took place on January 28, 1132, when it was used by Song General Han Shizhong to capture a city in Fujian, China. In Europe, the first mention of gunpowder's composition in express terms appeared in Roger Bacon's "De nullitate magiæ" at Oxford, published in 1216. Later, in 1248, his "Opus Maior" describes a recipe for gunpowder and recognized its military use: "We can, with saltpeter and other substances, compose artificially a fire that can be launched over long distances . . . By only using a very small quantity of this material much light can be created accompanied by a horrible fracas. It is possible with it to destroy a town or an army."

The direct ancestor of the gun is the fire lance, a black-powder-filled tube attached to the end of a spear and used as a flamethrower (quite different to the Byzantine flamethrower); shrapnel was sometimes placed in the barrel so that it would explode out together with the flames. The earliest illustration of a gunpowder weapon is the depiction of a fire-lance on a mid-twelfth century silk banner from Dunhuang, China. The proportion of saltpeter in the propellant was increased in due course to maximise its explosive power. To better withstand that explosive power, the paper and bamboo of which fire-lance barrels were originally made came to be replaced by metal. To take full advantage of that increased

Battle-Ax Gun

Duckfoot Pistol

power, the shrapnel was replaced by projectiles whose size and shape filled the barrel more closely—effectively the first "bullets." With this, we have the three basic features of the gun: a barrel made of metal, high-nitrate gunpowder, and a projectile which totally occludes the muzzle so that the powder charge exerts maximum propellant force, allowing for the projectile to be fired in a roughly targeted direction.

The earliest depiction of a gun is a sculpture from a cave in Sichuan, China, dating to the twelfth century, which shows a figure carrying a vase-shaped bombard with flames and a cannonball coming out of it. The oldest surviving gun, made of bronze, has been dated to 1288—it was discovered at a site in modern-day Acheng District of China.

By the later fourteenth century, hand-held firearms—hand cannons—made an appearance. When metal projectiles could pierce armor, chain mail became a necessity, yet often was a poor defense against gunpowder and metal. Soon hand-to-hand combat was used only as a last means of defense.

As deadly as these early weapons were, it would be several centuries before technological advances allowed hand guns to fire more than one projectile at a time. Guns did not cause the obsolescence of other weapons; knives, swords, and other implements were still needed in combat. To overcome the deficiency of single-fire weapons, combination weapons—those that could perform more than one function—were developed. Single-fire guns were fitted with bayonets, and the fighting ax contained a gun in the handle. If the shot missed the target, its user had an alternate defense source. Combination weapons continue

Thompson sub machine gun

to be manufactured today. A recent example would be a cellular phone that contains a small .22 caliber pistol that could be used for assassinations or easily smuggled through security screening by terrorists.

Multi-shot weapons appeared in the nineteenth century; early examples, called "pepper-boxes," shot from five to twenty times. Perhaps the most famous multi-shot weapon was the Gatling gun, capable of firing up to 800 rounds per minute, which—had it been introduced earlier—might have meant an earlier triumph by the Union Army during the U.S. Civil War. The twentieth century saw its share of multi-shot weapons; one of the best known was the Thompson sub-machine gun used by the likes of Roaring Twenties gangsters Dillinger and Bonnie and Clyde. Once it was adopted by the military, the multi-shooting machine gun changed warfare. With one-shot guns, advancement toward an enemy could be accomplished during reloading. With machine guns, movement on an open battlefield became more deadly, and gunplay was performed from entrenchments and behind barricades.

In the modern era, technology continues to change the way weapons function in society, yet today's weapons technology has not made firearms obsolete. The military use of precision guided missiles has changed the way modern armies accomplish their goals and objectives. Yet, firearms still play an important role in warfare.

In modern times, the country with the most weapons or the largest arsenal has the most military power, and military power symbolizes superior world status.

Aside from practical use, weapons have a unique appeal for collectors and museums because of their technology, materials, craftsmanship, and beauty. The most ordinary weapons tell the story of time and the society in which they were made and used. Though they served and continue to serve deadly purposes, weapons allow a glimpse into human history.

In the modern era, technology continues to change the way weapons function in society, yet today's weapons technology has not made firearms obsolete. The military use of precision guided missiles has changed the way modern armies accomplish their goals and objectives. Yet, firearms still play an important role in warfare.

Mao Zedong's statement that "Political power grows out of the barrel of a gun" is as true today as it was in 1938. The country with the largest arsenal has the most military power, and military power symbolizes superior world status.

Aside from practical use, weapons have a unique appeal for collectors and museums because of their technology, materials, craftsmanship, and beauty. The most ordinary weapons tell the story of time and the society in which they were made and used. Though they served and continue to serve deadly purposes, weapons allow a glimpse into human history.

Robert P. Lindley

ROBERT LINDLEY
COLLECTIONS MANAGER
BERMAN MUSEUM OF WORLD HISTORY
ANNISTON, ALABAMA

French Model 1937 Mortar Gun

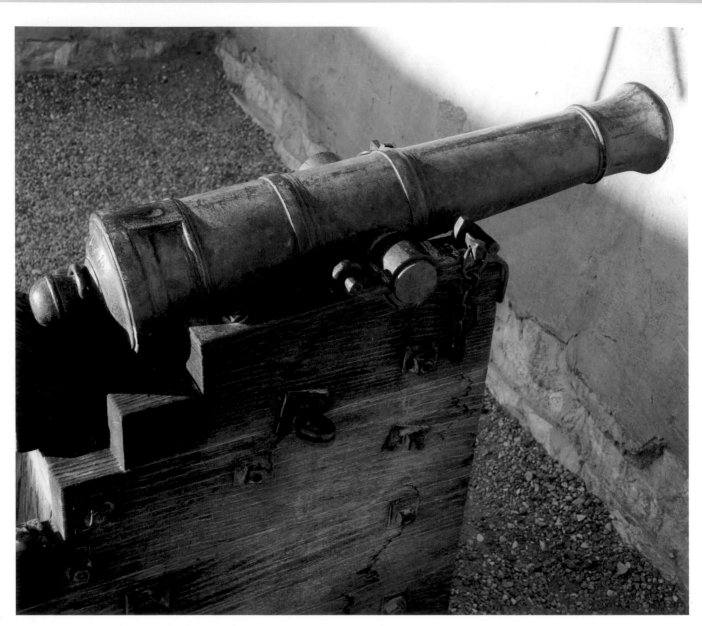

The Gunpowder Revolution

The term "gunpowder," or "black powder," refers to an explosive compound of charcoal, potassium nitrate (saltpeter), and sulfur. Its introduction into warfare—which, as best as can be determined, took place in fourteenth-century Europe—represented a huge advance in military technology: For the first time, energy to drive a projectile could be stored in chemical form, rather than in the form of human muscle power or by mechanical means. The so-called "Gunpowder Revolution" didn't happen overnight; it would take many years to develop truly effective gunpowder weapons and to figure out how to deploy them to optimum effect in battle, but the revolution's effects would be profoundly felt throughout the world.

FROM FIREWORKS TO FIREARMS

There are various theories about where and when black explosive powder was first "discovered" and how it was first applied to weaponry. Most historians agree that the substance was known in China as early as the tenth century, where it was apparently used in Taoist religious rituals, and later as fireworks and possibly as a means of signaling. Whether the Chinese made use of black-powder weapons over the next few centuries is still debated. Other's assert that Arab scientists may have made black powder during approximately the same period, or that Medieval European alchemists stumbled across the formula in their neverending quest to "transmute" base metals like lead into gold. It's also possible that explosive powder developed simultaneously in several societies over the course of a few centuries.

Sometime between the tenth and fourteenth centuries, came the discovery that black powder could propel a projectile from a tube. The earliest dated image of a gunpowder weapon in use appears in an illuminated European manuscript of 1326. It depicts a soldier touching a bar of heated iron to the base of a vase-shaped vessel, which discharges an arrow-like projectile.

Out of primitive weapons like this developed the cannon—an iron tube banded to a wooden frame, firing balls of iron or carved stone. Given the primitive metallurgy and chemistry of the time (a truly stable and storable version of gunpowder would not be developed until the seventeenth century), these early artillery pieces burst easily and were often more dangerous to the firer than to the target.

CASTLES UNDER SIEGE

The first use of cannon in battle is also debated. An account of the Battle of Crecy (1346) in the Hundred Years War between England and France describes the English army using "bombards" against the French, and cannon were also present at the Battle of Agincourt in 1415. Given the poor accuracy of these early cannon, their effectiveness on the battlefield was probably more psychological than anything else; belching smoke and flame with ear-splitting noise, a cannon hurling a projectile could knock a mounted knight off his horse or tear through an infantry formation (with a very lucky shot). These new weapons were terrifying to soldiers who had never before seen anything like them.

The most significant use of early artillery, however, was as siege weapons to batter down the castle walls and other fortifications. By the end of the fifteenth century, French and Italian gunmakers had developed relatively sturdy and easily transportable guns, and rulers like Louis XI of France (1423–

1483) and his successor Charles VII (1470–1498) skillfully exploited artillery both to consolidate their authority at home and conquer territory abroad.

While improvements in fortification eventually stymied the effectiveness of siege cannon, to an extent these weapons played an important role in facilitating the rise of the centralized nation-state in Europe. In the same era, the Ottoman Turkish Empire used massive siege guns—some so big they had to be manufactured on-site—to help destroy the walls of Constantinople (now Istanbul) in 1453, ending the thousand-year-old Byzantine Empire.

Around the turn of the fifteenth century, firearms intended for infantry troops began to appear on battlefields. Originally called hand cannons or hand gonnes (see pp 22–23), they were later known by a variety of terms, including the arquebus and, eventually, the musket, the latter term probably coming from the French *mosquette*. These muskets used the matchlock firing system, which was unreliable in damp conditions; as muzzle-loaders, they had a slow rate of fire; and as smoothbore weapons, they were accurate only at short distances, typically no more than 900ft/75m. The introduction of the flintlock firing system in the seventeenth century increased the musket's reliability, but the problems of slow firing and relative inaccuracy wouldn't be solved until the advent of breach-loading weapons and the widespread adoption of rifling in the nineteenth century.

"The main foundations of every state, new states as well as ancient or composite ones, are good laws and good arms—you cannot have good laws without good arms, and where there are good arms, good laws inevitably follow."

—Niccolo Machiavelli, from *The Prince*

Gunpowder's origins are somewhat mysterious. Cannon and bombs may have been used in Chinese warfare as early as the twelfth century, and their first reported use in Europe came around two centuries. Often firing balls of carved stone, early cannon were crude and dangerous to operate, but they were effective against fortifications and their use on battlefields must have had a powerful psychological effect. The development of handheld firearms had profound consequences, giving the infantry the upper hand in battle and ultimately ending the era of the mounted knight. By the eighteenth century, firearms technology had advanced from the matchlock arquebus to the flintlock musket, which—in the hands of drilled, disciplined, professional armies—came to dominate the battlefield. The "Gunpowder Revolution" also gave European soldiers an advantage over indigenous peoples as the Western powers built empires in what they called "the New World."

From Hand Cannon to Matchlock

Handheld gunpowder weapons—usually called hand cannons or hand gonnes—developed in parallel with artillery. They first appeared in Europe during the mid-fifteenth century and were basically just miniature cannons, held under a soldier's arm or braced against his shoulder—and often supported by a stake—with a second soldier firing the weapon by means of a slow match (see below). The introduction of the matchlock firing system led to the development of lighter, less awkward handheld guns that could be loaded and fired by one man, including the arquebus and its successor, the musket. In the next century, infantry equipped with matchlock-equipped guns would become a major component of armies in both Europe and Asia.

THE MATCHLOCK

The "match" in matchlock was actually a length of cord soaked in a chemical compound (usually potassium nitrate, aka saltpeter) to make it burn slowly. The match was held in an S-shaped lever (the serpentine) over a pan of priming powder. Pulling the trigger lowered the match, igniting the priming powder, which then (by means of a touch-hole) ignited the main powder charge in the barrel and fired the projectile. A later, spring-loaded variation, the snap lock, "snapped" the serpentine down into the pan.

Shoulder-fired matchlock guns—variously known as arquebuses, hackbuts, calivers, culverins, and eventually muskets—had many drawbacks, most notably their unreliability in wet weather and the fact that the smoldering match could betray the firer's position to the enemy. Despite their deficiencies, matchlock firearms proved remarkably enduring—largely because they were inexpensive to manufacture and simple to use.

CHINESE SIGNAL GUN

While the Chinese probably made the first use of gunpowder (see pp 12–13) as early as the tenth century, just when they applied gunpowder to weaponry is debated. The Chinese certainly made use of gunpowder for ceremonial purposes, for firecrackers, and for signaling purposes early on; shown here is a Chinese hand cannon, probably used for signaling, from the eighteenth century. It is made of bronze and decorated with a dragon stretching from breech to muzzle.

INDIAN TORADOR

The torador was a type of matchlock musket used in India for hundreds of years. This model, from the eighteenth or early nineteenth century, has a 46in/117cm barrel ending in a muzzle chiseled in the form of a leopard's head; the breach and muzzle feature koftgari decoration—a form of inlaying gold and steel.

SPANISH HAND CANNON

While hand cannons were usually braced against the chest or shoulder or held under the arm, this sixteenth-century Spanish weapon, just 5.5in/20cm in overall length, was fired literally from the hand—making it an early pistol. Made of bronze, the handle is in the form of a seated lion.

JAPANESE PISTOL

An eighteenth-century Japanese matchlock pistol. The first firearms came to Japan by way of Portuguese traders in the 1540s and were soon copied by native craftsmen. The Japanese took quickly to guns, with competing feudal lords equipping their soldiers with matchlock muskets (tanegashima). After the establishment of the Tokugawa Dynasty in 1603, however, production and possession of firearms was severely restricted in Japan.

BATTLE OF MORAT GUN

This hand cannon—which hints at the form factor of the later pistol—was captured by Swiss troops after the Battle of Morat, fought near Bern on June 22, 1476. The battle saw the outnumbered Swiss defeat the forces of Charles the Bold, the Duke of Burgundy. The battle was notable in being one of the first in which large numbers of handheld firearms were used; as many as 10,000 on both sides combined, according to some sources.

FRENCH HAND GONNE

An early French hand cannon, with a 1in/2.5cm barrel attached to a rough wooden stock with iron bands. This weapon eventually wound up in Morocco, North Africa.

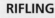

KEY PISTOL

Shown here is a highly unusual adaptation of the matchlock mechanism: A combination gate key and matchlock pistol from eighteenth-century Scotland. The key operated the gate of a castle; the gatekeeper carried the weapon in case an intruder attempted to break into the castle while the gate was being unlocked.

RIFLING

As early as the fifteenth century, European gunsmiths began boring grooves on the inside of gun barrels—a process that would become known as rifling. The initial purpose was probably to reduce the buildup of gunpowder residue in the barrel, but it was discovered that a barrel with spiral grooves gave stability to a bullet in flight, greatly increasing its accuracy. Rifling, however, was a difficult process until the improvements in technology brought by the Industrial Revolution. Although rifles were used in hunting and carried by specialist military units, most firearms remained smoothbore (i.e., nonrifled) until well into the nineteenth century.

From Matchlock to Flintlock

Despite its remarkable longevity, the matchlock's deficiencies led gunsmiths to experiment with better firing systems for handheld weapons. The next major advance in this field came with the introduction of the wheel-lock mechanism in the early sixteenth century, but this system was later supplanted by the flintlock mechanism. Widely adopted in Europe in the seventeenth century, the flintlock remained standard in much of the world until the introduction of the percussion cap system in the nineteenth century (see p 52).

THE WHEEL LOCK

The wheel lock combined a spring-loaded, serrated metal wheel and a dog, or cock—a pair of metal jaws that held a piece of iron pyrite. The wheel was wound up (usually with a key) to put tension on the spring. When the trigger was pulled, the cock struck against the rotating wheel, striking sparks to fire the weapon. Various conflicting theories abound of when, where, and how the wheel-lock gun developed, but it was likely inspired by the handheld tinder-lighters in use at the time.

The introduction of the wheel lock spurred the development of the pistol. (The term "pistol" may derive from the arms-producing city of Pistoia in Italy, although there are other theories; early pistols were often called dags, which probably derives from an old French word for "dagger.") Pistols put firepower into the hands of mounted troops; as concealable weapons, criminals and assassins also quickly adopted them. In 1584, a wheel-lock pistol was employed to murder the Dutch leader William the Silent in the world's first political assassination by pistol.

THE FLINTLOCK

The wheel lock's heyday was brief. By the mid- to late sixteenth century, Northern Europe saw the development of the snaphance, or snaphaunce, lock. (The term came from a Dutch word for "pecking bird.") In the snaphance, the cock held a piece of flint, which sprang forward on the trigger-pull to strike a piece of steel (the frizzen), sending sparks into the priming pan. A similar type of lock, the miquelet, appeared around the same time in Southern Europe. Technical refinements to both eventually led to the introduction of the true flintlock early in the seventeenth century.

GERMAN WHEEL-LOCK RIFLE

A German wheel-lock rifle, probably made in Nuremberg in 1597. The stock is inlaid with ivory carvings of deer and fowl. Wheel-lock muskets and rifles were expensive, so they enjoyed much popularity as hunting weapons for the aristocracy and the rich.

THE KENTUCKY RIFLE

A weapon steeped in American history and folklore, the Kentucky rifle (or long rifle) was first produced by immigrant German gunsmiths in Pennsylvania, Virginia, and other colonies in the mid-eighteenth century. (The designation "Kentucky rifle" was popularized in a song, "The Hunters of Kentucky," which celebrated the marksmanship of volunteers from that state in the Battle of New Orleans on January 8, 1815.) German gunsmiths had long produced rifled weapons, but the traditional German hunting rifle was relatively short, with a barrel of about 30in/76cm.

In America, gunsmiths began lengthening the barrel to between 40in/101cm and 46in/117cm, greatly increasing its accuracy. The resulting weapon, typically .50, proved ideal for hunting in the North American wilderness. They were handsome weapons as well, usually with stocks of curly maple and often beautifully decorated. Formations of riflemen recruited from the frontier fought against the British in the Revolutionary War and in the War of 1812. Although capable of dealing death at long distances (during the Revolutionary War, an astonished British officer reported that a rifleman hit his bugler's horse at a range of 400yd/366m), the long rifle was even slower to reload than the smoothbore musket, a fact that limited its effectiveness in conventional battle.

Originally flintlock, many long rifles were later converted to percussion (see pp 56–57), including the two examples shown here; the lower one was made by the Lemans of Lancaster County, Pennsylvania, a family of prominent gunsmiths active from the mid-1700s to around 1875.

"For 'tis not often here you see A hunter from Kentucky."

—lyrics from "The Hunters of Kentucky," 1824

RAMPART GUN

A wheel-lock European rampart gun from about 1600. Rampart guns were mounted on the walls of castles and fortifications (and, at sea, on ship's rails) for defense; this .76 model was designed so that it could be fired by "remote control" by means of a string.

GERMAN WHEEL-LOCK PISTOLS

This rare and magnificent pair of wheel-lock pistols was made in Saxony, Germany, around 1590. They are shown with a matched box designed to carry five cartridges—which at the time consisted of powder and ball wrapped in paper or leather—and the key required to wind the wheel-lock mechanism.

INDIAN BLUNDERBUSS

An eighteenth-century Indian flintlock blunderbuss (see pp 40–41) pistol with silver damascening on the barrel. This gun has a "swamped" barrel, which tapers to a flared muzzle.

CAMEL GUN

An eighteenth-century Arab flintlock musket with an engraved lock plate, ivory butt plate, and silver barrel bands. Sometimes called camel guns from their use in mounted warfare and raiding, muskets of this type were carried by some Arab and Berber warriors until late in the nineteenth century.

CANNON IGNITER

Flintlock mechanisms were used not only on handheld guns, but were also fitted to artillery, particularly naval guns. Shown here is a British flintlock cannon igniter from the early nineteenth century. The 22in/56cm weapon's lock was placed against the touch-hole of a cannon; pulling the trigger pulled back an external link that fired it and ignited the powder charge.

PERSIAN PISTOL

A beautiful Persian flintlock pistol of the eighteenth century. Instead of being inlaid or engraved, the beautiful gold decoration is overlaid.

AFRICAN TRADE GUNS

Guns were a major factor in the slave trade that brought some 10 million Africans to the Americas in bondage (with untold deaths along the way) from the fifteenth through the nineteenth centuries. European slavers exchanged guns, and other goods, with West African tribal leaders; these guns were then used in intertribal warfare to capture more slaves to sell. The .72 musket shown here was made for African export in the eighteenth century, although the barrel was apparently manufactured in Italy much earlier.

FRENCH MUSKET

This French military musket made in 1813 and shown with its bayonet, is typical of the last generation of smoothbore flintlock long arms. Within a couple of decades they would be replaced by rifled weapons using the percussion-cap (see p 52) firing system.

GERMAN WHEEL-LOCK MUSKET

Another finely made example of a wheel lock weapon.

SUNDIAL GUN

Made in 1788, this "gun" uses the
heat of the sun's rays, rather than any type of
lock, to fire. The purpose of these so-called sundial
guns was to announce the arrival of noon. Aligned on a
north-south axis, the lens was adjusted, according to the season, to
focus the sun's rays on a powder charge, which discharged a small gun
when the sun was directly overhead—i.e., at noon.

This implement was mostly used shipboard, as the sound carried well
over the water, but the sundial gun had its detractors. In an edition of Poor
Richard's Almanac, Ben Franklin found this contraption an attractive target:
"How to make a STRIKING SUNDIAL, by which not only a Man's own
Family, but all his Neighbours for ten Miles round, may know what o'Clock
it is, when the Sun shines, without seeing the Dial. [. . .] Note also, That the
chief Expence will be the Powder, for the Cannon once bought, will, with
Care, last 100 Years. Note moreover, That there will be a great Saving of
Powder in cloudy Days. Kind Reader, Methinks I hear thee say, That it is
indeed a good Thing to know how the Time passes."

COEHORN MORTAR

A mortar is a short-barrelled cannon that fires projectiles in an arching
trajectory—"plunging fire," in military terminology, as opposed to the
"direct fire" of conventional cannon. They were ideal for siege warfare
because they could lob an exploding shell (a hollow projectile filled with
gunpowder and fitted with a fuse before firing) over the walls of a castle or
fort. Early mortars were often massive and crude weapons, but in the late
seventeenth century the Dutch military engineer Menno van Coehorn (1641–
1704) invented a compact, lightweight mortar that could be carried close to
the target by a crew of two to four men. Mortars of the Coehorn type
remained in use well into the nineteenth century; shown here is an English
example from the early eighteenth century. The Coehorn is the ancestor of
the mortars used for infantry support in all contemporary armies.

ARAB MIQUELET

An Arab flintlock gun using a snaphance-style mechanism. The stock is inlaid with silver wire and, as with many guns from North Africa and the Middle East, the buttstock is of finely carved ivory.

VOLLEY GUN

Volley guns—weapons with multiple barrels, all of which discharged simultaneously—were used in close-in naval fighting to repel boarders. The most famous of these guns is probably the Nock volley gun shown here. (While the famous British gunsmith Henry Nock made the weapon, he was apparently not the designer.) First appearing around 1780, the flintlock gun had seven 20in/51cm .50 rifled barrels. Some 600 were produced for the Royal Navy. While obviously a formidable weapon, it had its downside: The recoil was said to be severe enough to break the firer's shoulder, and the muzzle blast sometimes set sails and rigging on fire. The weapon is familiar to modern readers of Bernard Cornwell's popular series of historical novels set during the Napoleonic Wars, in which it is carried (on land) by one of the main characters.

DEATH BATTERY

Known as "death organs," or "organ guns," because their rows of barrels resemble a rack of organ pipes, weapons like the one shown here—which dates from the seventeenth century—were an early form of multishot firearm. This example has 15 barrels, each 17.5in/44cm long fixed to a wooden base. Organ guns evolved into battery guns, which were used to defend bridges and other vulnerable locations in conflicts up until the American Civil War.

The Flintlock Pistol

The adoption of the flintlock firing mechanism (see p 24) led to a proliferation of pistols. Despite their considerable drawbacks—ineffectiveness at any but close ranges, slow loading by the muzzle, vulnerability to inclement weather—these guns gave individuals a potent weapon for self-defense, which was no small thing in an era without the benefit of any organized police forces, and in which robbers lurked after dark on the streets of towns and cities and highwaymen haunted rural roads.

COAT, HOLSTER, AND BELT PISTOLS

Generally, pistols of the flintlock era fall into three types:

The first were coat pistols, also known as traveler's pistols. As the name implies, these were personal-defense weapons compact enough to be carried in the pockets of the overcoats worn by men of the time; very short-barreled versions could also be carried in a waistcoat pocket or elsewhere on one's person.

The second type were holster, or horse pistols—relatively long-barreled weapons intended to be worn in a holster attached to a horse's saddle.

The third type were belt pistols. Of an intermediate size and caliber between coat and holster pistols, they were usually fitted with a hook, which could be attached to the belt.

TURN-OFFS AND TURN-OVERS

While a majority of flintlock pistols were muzzle-loaders, like their long-arm counterparts, the so-called turn-off, or screw-off pistol appeared in the mid-seventeenth century. These weapons had a cannon-shaped barrel (see the example on p 82) that could be unscrewed, loaded with a bullet, and replaced; the powder charge went into a compartment in the breech. In contrast to the mostly smoothbore pistols of the time, turn-offs often had rifled barrels, greatly increasing accuracy. During the English Civil Wars (1642–51), Prince Rupert, commander of the Royalist cavalry, is said to have used

such a weapon to hit the weathervane atop a church at a distance about 300ft/91m; he then repeated the shot to prove the first was not a fluke.

There were also multiple-barreled pistols. One type had two side-by-side barrels, each fired by a separate lock; another, the turn-over pistol, had two or more barrels that were loaded individually and rotated into place to be fired by a single lock. Gunsmiths also tried flintlock pepperboxes and even revolvers (see pp 56–57, 62); however, most multiple-shot flintlock pistols tended to be unreliable and prone to accidental firing. An exception was the duckfoot pistol (see the example below), which had several barrels in a horizontal configuration designed for simultaneous firing.

This fascinating selection of flintlocks features both rare and significant items from the fifteenth through nineteenth centuries.

BALKAN AX-PISTOL
Another ax-pistol combination, this one made in the Balkans in the eighteenth century. The stock is inlaid with silver wire in traditional Balkan designs.

TINDER LIGHTER
Though not a gun, this tinder lighter}s design was based on the flintlock mechanism and was used to start fires with wood shavings or chips. The sparks were created by the friction of the flint against metal. Made around 1820, this item predates the match.

PISTOL-SWORD
A rare sword-pistol combination from the mid-eighteenth century. Weapons like these were apparently used mainly by marines and naval officers in boarding engagements at sea (see pp 42–43).

GERMAN AX-PISTOL
Made in the Central European region of Silesia in the seventeenth century, this weapon combines a flintlock pistol with a battle-ax. Its decorative elements include an elephant stamped into the lock and a stock inlaid with bone.

BALKAN DRESS PISTOL
Also from the Balkans, this interesting pistol is not a weapon at all— while it resembles a typical locally made pistol, right down to its elaborate decoration and "rat-tail" butt, it lacks a functioning lock. Balkan nobles and warriors of the sixteenth and seventeenth centuries were required by custom to carry pistols, but this led to a spate of assassinations. As a compromise, non-functioning pistols like the one shown here were worn at meetings and on ceremonial occasions: They satisfied dress requirements, but put no one in danger.

DUCKFOOT PISTOL
"Duckfoot" pistols—like the four-barreled version shown here, made by the London shop of Goodwin & Co.—were multiple-barreled weapons, so-called because the angled barrels resembled a duck's web. In popular legend, at least, they were favorites of sea captains and prison warders, because they could be used to keep a mutinous crew or rioting prisoners at bay.

COAT PISTOL
A short-barreled coat pistol, probably made in France around the turn of the nineteenth century.

DOG HEAD PISTOL
Another French coat pistol, this one with a butt carved in the form of a fierce dog's head.

DUBLIN CASTLE PISTOL
This walnut-stocked, brass-finished .65 pistol was made in Dublin, Ireland, and bears the royal cipher of King George III (1738–1820). Ireland was a British colony at the time, and the armory at Dublin Castle was—together with the armories at Birmingham and at the Tower of London in England—a principal supplier of arms to the British army and navy.

CLERMONT PISTOL
A very finely made .48 pistol, probably French in origin.

GUARD PISTOLS
A pair of British Model 1796 holster pistols. Tower of London markings indicate that they were issued to the Royal Horse Guards regiment.

SQUARE BARREL
This early nineteenth century British pistol is unusual in having square barrel designed to fire matching bullets. The bullets produced more ragged—and thus more fatal—entry and exit wounds.

SCOTTISH RAM HORN PISTOLS

Scottish gunsmiths produced a number of unique designs during the flintlock era. Many Scottish pistols were made entirely of steel, and they often featured butts carved in a variety of shapes. The belt pistol shown here, made about 1780, is representative: Of all-steel construction, it has a "ram's head" butt; a pricker (used to clear powder residue from the touch-hole) screws in between the "horns."

FRENCH PISTOLS

A pair of eighteenth century French pistols, manufactured (or at least assembled) at the Royal Armory at Maubeuge, which was founded in 1718 along with arsenals at St. Etienne and Charleville.

CANNON BARREL PISTOL

A .52 cannon-barreled pistol made by Patrick of Liverpool around 1805. This type of pistol got its name from the resemblance of their barrels to those of artillery pieces; they were also known as "Queen Anne pistols," although according to firearms historian David Miller, most were produced well after that British queen's death in 1714. The pistol also uses a boxlock action, in which the firing mechanism is located on top of the breech rather than on the side of the weapon.

SPANISH BELT PISTOL
A .70 Spanish belt pistol from around 1740. The weapon uses a miquelet lock (see p 24).

ITALIAN PISTOLS
A matched pair of Italian pistols, likely made in Turin (Torino) in the early nineteenth century.

Dueling Pistols

Combat between individuals to settle disputes over personal honor is as old as history, but the practice of dueling familiar to us today developed in Southern Europe during the Renaissance, and began to flourish—largely among the upper classes—in Europe and North America in the eighteenth century. Although widely outlawed and denounced (George Washington forbade his officers to fight duels, calling it a "murderous practice"), dueling continued in Britain and America into the early nineteenth century, and somewhat later in Continental Europe. Until the mid-1700s, duelists fought mainly with swords, but the fashion moved to firearms, creating a new class of weapon—the dueling pistol.

THE GREAT GUNSMITHS

Originally, duelists used ordinary pistols, but around 1770, gunsmiths—chiefly in England and France—began producing purpose-built dueling pistols. These were usually made as "cased pairs"—two identical pistols in a box with powder flasks, bullet molds, and other accessories. With dueling mainly an upper-class custom (in Europe at least), owning a costly cased set of dueling pistols was a status symbol—like driving a high-powered sports car today. The pistols produced by the most famous (and expensive) London gunsmiths—like Robert Wogdon and the rival brothers John and Joseph Manton—were, in this sense, the Ferraris and Porsches of their time.

ACCURACY AND RELIABILITY

Most dueling pistols were approximately 15 inches long with 10-inch- barrels; the usual caliber was between .40 and .50. They were extremely accurate at about twenty yards—the usual distance at which duelists fired—although the commonly accepted rules of dueling stipulated smoothbore barrels and only the simplest sights. (Some duelists cheated by rifling all but the last couple of inches of the barrel—a practice known as "blind rifling.")

For maximum accuracy, many dueling pistols featured a "set" or "hair" trigger. The set trigger utilized a mechanism that kept tension on the trigger so that only a slight pressure would fire the weapon. (Conventional triggers required a heavy pull that tended to distort the firer's aim.)

Besides accuracy, reliability was the duelist's paramount concern in a pistol, so all components were finely tooled and fitted. In contrast to many firearms of the era, most dueling pistols had only minimal ornamentation, so that sunlight gleaming off gold or silver inlay wouldn't distract the duelist. Continental gunsmiths, however, did make some richly ornamented dueling pistols, and elaborately inlaid and engraved cased pairs were often produced as presentation pieces not intended for actual use on the "field of honor."

CARON'S CASE

France's royal gunmaker, Alphonse Caron of Paris, made this cased set of pistols in the late 1840s. The case contains the standard accessories—powder flask, bullet mold, ramrods, cleaning rods, and boxes for percussion caps. The powder flask is decorated with Egyptian hieroglyphics—a reflection of the popularity of ancient Egyptian motifs in nineteenth-century France.

RARE PAIR
This set of Belgian-made, percussion .44 dueling pistols came with unusual accessories—hand guards that fitted over the lock and trigger guard. For training purposes, the pistols could be made to fire wax bullets (thus the hand guards for protection).

WOGDON PISTOL
This pistol by the celebrated English gunsmith Robert Wogdon could be fitted with a wooden shoulder stock for non-dueling use. Originally a flintlock, it was later converted to percussion action. Wogdon made the pistols used in the famous 1804 duel in which Vice President Aaron Burr mortally wounded his personal and political enemy Alexander Hamilton.

BELGIAN PISTOLS
Flintlock dueling pistols had all the disadvantages of the flintlock system—they misfired frequently, were unreliable in damp conditions, and the relative slowness of the firing mechanism hampered accuracy even with the use of set triggers (see main text). After 1815 (just as dueling was on the wane), makers of dueling pistols—like the Belgian gunsmith who produced the handsome pair above—increasingly switched to the more robust and reliable percussion-cap system.

The Blunderbuss

The blunderbuss was a short, usually flintlock, smoothbore musket with a barrel that ended in a flared muzzle. The weapon developed in Europe, probably in Germany at first, early in the seventeenth century, although it didn't come into widespread use until about a hundred years later. (The weapon got its name from the Anglicization of a Dutch term *donderbuse*, meaning "thunder-box" or "thunder-gun.") Firing lead shot, the blunderbuss was deadly at short range and was generally used as a defensive weapon—by coachmen against highwaymen, by merchants and homeowners against burglars, and by innkeepers against robbers. It was also used at sea, as it was an ideal weapon in a boarding attack.

THE "THUNDER-BOX"

There are a couple of popular misconceptions about the blunderbuss. The first is that its flared muzzle (often described as bell-shaped or trumpet-shaped) served to scatter its load of shot in the manner of a modern shotgun. In fact, the dispersal pattern for the shot was little different than that of a nonflared barrel. The muzzle's wide mouth, however, facilitated quick reloading. It also had a psychological effect. In the words of firearms historian Richard Akehurst, "[T]he great bell mouth was most intimidating: those at whom it was aimed were convinced that there was no escaping the dreadful blast." Akehurst also notes that some English blunderbuss owners upped the intimidation factor by having the inscription "Happy is he that escapeth me" engraved on the barrel.

The second misconception is that blunderbuss was often loaded not with conventional shot but with scrap metal, nails, stones, gravel, or even broken glass for a particularly devastating effect. This may have happened on occasion, but such loads would quickly ruin the weapon's barrel.

ON THE ROAD AND OFF

The Blunderbuss's heyday was in the eighteenth century, when more and more people were traveling the primitive roads of Europe, and the danger of being waylaid by pistol-wielding highwaymen was always present. The blunderbuss's barrel was usually made of nonrusting brass—a necessity as they were often carried by coach drivers and guards who sat exposed to the weather.

Besides its use at sea—by both the regular naval forces and by pirates and privateers—the blunderbuss saw some military service on land. The Austrian, British, and Prussian armies of the eighteenth century all fielded units armed with the weapon, and according to some sources, the American Continental Army considered adopting the blunderbuss in preference to the carbine for its mounted troops during the Revolutionary War. However, the blunderbuss's very short range limited its effectiveness in a conventional combat role.

The blunderbuss remained popular into the early decades of the nineteenth century, when the shotgun replaced it as the preferred short-range defensive firearm.

TRAP GUN

Made for hunting rather than for offense or defense against human targets, this nineteenth-century European percussion-cap trap gun utilizes a blunderbuss-style barrel. Trap guns were connected by string or wire to a baited trap; when the animal took the bait, the string or wire tripped the trigger and discharged the gun.

FRENCH

While most blunderbusses had musket-type shoulder stocks, eighteenth- and nineteenth-century gunsmiths also produced blunderbuss pistols, like the French weapon shown here. They were often carried by French naval officers, and were also used widely in the street fighting that accompanied the French Revolution.

INDIAN

This eighteenth-century Indian blunderbuss differs from its European counterparts in that it has a steel rather than a brass barrel and uses matchlock ignition, a system long obsolete in Europe and the Americas. The 11in/28cm barrel is decorated with a fish-scale pattern. The needle-like object attached to the gun is a touch-hole pricker, used to clear gunpowder residue from the vent that communicated the match's flame to the powder charge.

AMERICAN

The U.S. government arsenal at Harper's Ferry, Virginia, produced this blunderbuss in 1814. Like other nations, the United States produced blunderbusses for use by sailors and marines and also as rampart guns for forts on land. Meriwether Lewis and William Clark also took a pair of blunderbusses with them on their famous exploring expedition in the American West (1804–1806).

TURKISH

This finely decorated blunderbuss was presented to French general Aimable-Jean-Jacques Pélissier, later the Duke de Malakoff, by his wife. He may have had it with him at the Siege of Sevastopol during the Crimean War (1854–55).

EUROPEAN

A particularly short-barreled example of the blunderbuss, probably made early in the ninteenth century. Some of the best gunsmiths of the era—like Henry Nock (1741–1804) of Birmingham and London, England—produced blunderbusses.

Naval Weapons

From ancient times until well into the sixteenth century, naval warfare in the Western World was, in a sense, an extension of land fighting. Sea battles were typically fought close to shore by fleets of oar-propelled galleys. The object was to ram the enemy with the galley's fortified bow or otherwise get close enough to grapple with the enemy vessel. Then soldiers armed with conventional infantry weapons—spears, swords, and bows—would board the opposing galley to fight on deck. By the mid-seventeenth century, however, the sailing ship had evolved into a stable platform for heavy cannon. In the resulting Age of Sail, which lasted until the introduction of steam power two hundred years later, large-scale naval battles saw lines (columns) of warships battering each other with cannon at ranges of 300ft/122m or less, each side hoping to break the other's line and disable its ships. Many smaller actions between individual ships, however, were still decided by clashes between boarders and defenders, both armed with a variety of hand-held weapons.

THE BROADSIDE

Heavy guns had been mounted on European ships as early as the fourteenth century, but they were placed in "castles" on the main deck and they were limited in number and usefulness. During the reign of King Henry VIII (from 1509 to 1547), English warships began mounting cannon on lower decks, firing through gunports that could be closed when not in action. This began the evolution that ultimately led to the massive "ships of the line" of the Napoleonic Wars (see pp 48–51). These vessels carried as many as 136 guns on two to four decks.

The muzzle-loading, brass or iron-barreled ship's guns of the time were rated by the weight of the shot they fired, with 24- and 32-pounders the most common sizes. Round shot made of iron was the usual projectile, but specialized shot like chain shot (two small round shot joined by a length of chain, intended to tear the enemy's sails and rigging) were also used. In addition to these "long guns," warships of the era also carried carronades, or "smashers"— shorter guns that fired the same weight of shot, for use at close range.

The weight of a broadside (the combined weight of shot fired by all the guns on one side of a ship in a single volley) was devastating. The broadside weight of the Royal Navy's HMS *Victory* (flagship of Admiral Horatio Nelson at the Battle of Trafalgar in 1805) was 1150lb/522kg.

BOARDERS AWAY!

Warships in the Age of Sail usually also had a contingent of marines; in battle, these "sea soldiers" would take to the fighting tops (platforms on the masts) to fire at enemy sailors with muskets and—if the range was close enough— to throw grenades onto the enemy vessel's deck. If the ship came alongside its opponent, both marines and sailors would make up a boarding party, armed with weapons that could include pikes, cutlasses (short curved swords, also called hangers), blunderbusses (see pp 40–41), musketoons (short-barreled muskets), and pistols. Because it was virtually impossible to reload a muzzle-loading firearm in a pitched on-deck battle, guns were reversed and used as clubs after being fired.

GRENADE LAUNCHER

An interesting eighteenth-century British naval weapon, this "hand mortar" was used to fire a kind of incendiary grenade. A wooden projectile with one end soaked in pitch (an inflammable resin) and topped with a burning scrap of rag was inserted into the barrel: The weapon was then fired, lofting the flaming projectile onto the deck or into the rigging of an enemy ship in hopes of setting the vessel ablaze.

BELGIAN PISTOL

A .74 Belgian naval pistol, manufactured around 1810, according to the proof marks on the barrel.

RAIL GUN

A rare ship's rail gun from an Austrian warship. The weapon consisted of a 66in/168cm section of ship's rail with ten pistol barrels mounted vertically. (Three barrels are missing.) Each barrel was loaded individually, with priming powder for all distributed in a channel inside the rail. The idea was to ignite the charge and fire all the barrels at the moment an enemy boarding party tried to board. Its actual effectiveness is not known.

"On the right and left two seas enclose you, without even a single ship for escape; […] the Alps behind, scarcely passed by you when fresh and vigorous, hem you in. Here, soldiers, where you have first met the enemy, you must conquer or die."

—Hannibal, in an address to his troops, 218 BCE

The period from the Battle of Waterloo in 1815 to the outbreak of World War I ninety-nine years later saw weapons technology advance in leaps and bounds. By the mid-nineteenth century, the old smoothbore musket had given way to the rifle, a weapon of much greater range and accuracy. The flintlock firing mechanism was replaced, first by the percussion cap system, and later by weapons firing fully enclosed metallic cartridges.

The introduction of such cartridges made repeating weapons—which could fire multiple shots without reloading—a practical proposition, and by the end of the nineteenth century, most armies would be equipped with bolt-action, magazine-fed rifles. The revolver, popularized by Samuel Colt at mid-century, gave individuals a potent pistol, and inventors had developed automatic pistols by the end of the 1800s. The last years of the nineteenth century also saw the invention of the machine gun by Sir Hiram Maxim—a weapon that fired continuously as long as the trigger was pulled. With firearms now completely dominating the battlefield, edged weapons like swords were increasingly relegated to purely ceremonial roles, except in parts of the world that remained relatively untouched by Western technology.

Weapons of the Napoleonic Wars

On July 14, 1789, a Parisian mob stormed the Bastille prison—an infamous symbol of royal power—sparking the French Revolution and setting off a series of events that plunged Europe, and eventually much of the world, into war. Out of France's revolutionary chaos emerged a leader, Napoleon Bonaparte, whose astonishing success as a military commander formed the foundation of his political power. The Napoleonic Wars—which lasted from 1799 until the Emperor's final defeat at Waterloo in 1815—did not see any extraordinary technological leaps in weaponry, but Napoleon masterfully exploited the existing weapons of the day to conquer much of Europe.

INFANTRY WEAPONS

The standard infantry weapon of the Napoleonic Wars was the smoothbore, muzzle-loading flintlock musket (see p 27). Napoleon's infantrymen typically carried the .69 Charleville musket, named for the armory at Ardennes where the weapon was first produced in 1777. Among Napoleon's enemies, the British used the venerable .75 Land Pattern musket, known popularly as the "Brown Bess," the Prussian Army was equipped after 1809 with a .75 musket based largely on the French Charleville, while the Russian Army made use of a variety of imported and domestically produced muskets of various calibers before standardizing, around 1809, on a 17.78mm weapon.

The smoothbore musket was inherently inaccurate, with an effective range of no more than 300ft/90m. Accuracy wasn't a factor in the tactics of the time, however, which relied on massed formations of infantry firing in volleys to send, in effect, a "wall of lead" at the opposing line. If the enemy broke ranks in the face of this intense fire, a bayonet charge usually followed, but the bayonet's effect was mostly psychological.

All armies of the time had units which carried the much more accurate rifle, but because rifles were even slower to load than muskets, their use was largely limited to these specialized and often elite troops. The best-known rifle of the time was the Baker rifle, designed by London gunsmith Ezekiel Baker and introduced in the British Army around 1800. In 1809, in Spain, a British rifleman using a Baker killed a French general from a distance that may have been as much as 1,800ft/550m.

BRITISH CARBINE
An early eighteenth-century British Flintlock Carbine. The carbine has an early model brass trigger guard and butt plate, side plate, and ramrod pipe. The weapon is fitted with a trapped Swivel Ram Rod and bayonet.

NAPOLEONIC ARTILLERY

Napoleon began his military career as an artilleryman, and during his reign the French Army's artillery gained a reputation for excellence. This was particularly true of the horse artillery units, which were equipped with relatively light and mobile cannons (like the brass-barreled piece shown here) that could be rapidly moved into position and used in direct support of infantry. These weapons would fire round shot—solid iron balls—or, at closer ranges, canister shot, which consisted of scores of small metal balls that burst from the cannon's muzzle. Historians debate the effectiveness of Napoleonic artillery: Some contend it was the deadliest weapon, overall, in many battles; others argue that, like the bayonet, artillery fire served mainly to demoralize the enemy.

BRONZE ARTILLERY CANNON

With advances in construction and the use of bronze, the French were able to make a cannon such as this specimen that was half the weight of models of thirty years earlier. This greatly increased the mobility of the weapon, thus enabling more frequent usage.

CAVALRY WEAPONS

Mounted forces of Napoleonic-era armies were divided between light and heavy cavalry. Both carried swords, usually sabers designed for slashing, although the French retained a preference for "running through" their opponents with the point of their swords. Light cavalry often fought dismounted using carbines or pistols. Heavy cavalry, like the French Army's cuirassiers, usually fought from the saddle and were armed with heavy, straight-bladed swords.

The French Army also made use of mounted troops armed with lances, as did its opponents in the Russian, Prussian, and Austrian forces. Lancers were often pitted against infantry formations, because their lances could outdistance a bayonet thrust.

Edged weapons weren't limited to mounted troops. Officers of all military branches continued to carry swords, and noncommissioned officers in several armies carried pikes.

A NATION AT ARMS

Napoleon Bonaparte's success on the battlefield was due not to any great technological innovation in weaponry, but rather to his brilliance as a commander—and to his ruthless exploitation of available manpower. During the French Revolution, the relatively small professional army of the Bourbon regime was replaced by an army of conscripts—the famous Levée en Masse. Napoleon appropriated the innovation of conscription to his own dictatorial ends, drafting about 2.5 million Frenchmen into military service between 1804 and 1813. The Emperor's profligacy with the lives of his soldiers was legendary—as he told Count Metternich of Austria, "You can't stop me. I spend 30,000 men a month."

BRITISH PISTOLS

In 1796, the British Army introduced the New Land Pattern .65 holster pistol for cavalry use, although the pistol was not manufactured in large numbers until 1802. The weapon incorporated a swivel ramrod (visible on the upper pistol in this photo), which simplified loading while in the saddle. The lower pistol is a modified version.

THREE-SHOT PISTOL

This volley pistol bears similarities with a duckfoot pistol and shoots all of its rounds at the same time. It has a percussion cap mechanism and was made in Europe in the early nineteenth century.

AIR RIFLE

One of the most unusual weapons used during the Napoleonic Wars were the air rifles fielded by the Austrian Army in 1808–09. Weapons using compressed air to fire a projectile (similar to the one pictured above) were introduced in the seventeenth century, and they had obvious advantages over gunpowder; the air weapon makes little sound and produces no smoke or muzzle flash to give away the firer's position. These qualities made them ideal for sniping. The Austrian weapon known as the windbüchse (German for "wind rifle") was first made by Bartolomeo Girandoni around 1780. Reports of the gun's specifications vary, but it could apparently discharge a .51 or .52 bullet at speeds of up to 1000ft/305m per second—and it could get off twenty rounds on a single charge of compressed air. At first windbüchse were parceled out to conventional infantry units, but eventually the Austrians formed a special unit armed solely with the weapon. While the use of the windbüchse wasn't enough to defeat French troops, the fear they inspired reportedly led Napoleon himself to authorize the summary execution of any Austrian soldier found carrying one. Despite its effectiveness, the air rifle never caught on as a military weapon—probably because of the time-consuming pumping process needed to produce the necessary air-pressure, plus their reputation as "terror weapons."

DRUMMER BOY RIFLE

Picked up on the field after the Battle of Waterloo, this musket was carried by a French drummer boy; the weapon is 34.5in/88cm in length overall, in contrast to the 60in/152cm of the standard French Charleville musket, with a similarly downsized bayonet. It was later converted from a flintlock to percussion cap firing mechanism (see pp 56–57).

From Flintlock to Percussion Cap

By the turn of the nineteenth century, the flintlock (see pp 24–25) had been the standard firing mechanism for guns for more than a century. The flintlock's deficiencies—its vulnerability to inclement weather, and the delay between the ignition of the powder in the priming pan and the main charge—led several inventors to develop firing systems that used the strike of a hammer on chemical compounds, like fulminate of mercury, as the means of ignition. First implemented mainly on sporting guns, the percussion system (sometimes called the caplock) came into widespread military use in the mid-nineteenth century.

EARLY PERCUSSION WEAPONS

The percussion system was inspired by a sportsman's frustration. A Scottish clergyman, the Rev. Alexander Forsyth, realized that the interval between the trigger pull and the actual firing of his fowling piece gave birds enough of a warning to fly away. Around 1805, Forsyth developed a new lock in which a hammer struck a firing pin inserted into a small bottle containing a special detonating charge, which in turn fired the powder charge in the barrel. Forsyth's "scent bottle" lock, as it was called from its shape, was a major advance, although weapons based on the system had their drawbacks, like the possibility of the entire "bottle" exploding. But it inspired several gunsmiths—including notables like Joseph Manton, to work on alternative systems, especially after Forsyth's British patent expired in 1821. In the words of firearms historian Richard Akehurst, a variety of percussion-fired "pills, tapes, tubes, and caps" containing several different types of detonating compounds came into use.

THE PERCUSSION CAP

The variety that ultimately won widespread adoption was a metallic cap—first made of steel, later of copper—filled with a compound based around fulminate of mercury. The cap was placed on a nipple in the lock and was struck by a hammer when the firer pulled the trigger.

There is some debate about how and when the metallic percussion cap was developed, but it's generally credited to a British-born American artist and inventor, Joshua Shaw (1776–1860), who developed it around 1814 but did not patent it until several years later. While some other percussion systems came into use—like the tape-primer system introduced in the 1840s by American inventor Edward Maynard (1813–1891), which operated much like a contemporary toy cap pistol—the stand-alone metallic cap became standard from the 1820s onward. The percussion system's popularity was helped by the relative ease with which flintlock weapons could be converted to the new mechanism.

The percussion system's advantages over the flintlock were considerable. It was reliable in all weathers and far less prone to misfire. The system also facilitated the introduction of reliable repeating weapons, especially the revolver (see pp 62–69). Still, it took several decades for the percussion system to win acceptance in military circles. (Napoleon Bonaparte was reportedly interested in developing weapons based on the Forsyth system, but the patriotic reverend rebuffed the French dictator's overtures.) It was not until the early 1840s, when the British Army began retrofitting its muskets with percussion locks, that percussion weapons became standard in the armies of the day.

The heyday of the percussion cap was relatively brief. Percussion firearms still had the drawbacks of muzzle-loading weapons, and after the introduction of self-contained metallic cartridges starting in the 1850s (see p 66), they rapidly gave way to cartridge-firing weapons.

HARPER'S FERRY

In 1841 the other major U.S. arsenal—at Harper's Ferry, Virginia—began producing a new smoothbore percussion musket. The Springfield and Harper's Ferry arsenals together turned out about 175,000 Model 1842 muskets (like the one shown here) before 1855, when a rifled version was introduced. Many Model 1842's were returned to the arsenals to have their barrels rifled to take the new Minié ball ammunition (see p 71).

SPRINGFIELD

The .69 U.S. Army Model 1835 Musket, manufactured at the government armory at Springfield, Massachusetts, was among the last smoothbore long arms in official U.S. military service. Some 30,000 were made between 1835 and 1844. Originally flintlocks, these muskets were converted to percussion starting in the late 1840s. The detail shows the lock with the hammer down on the nipple on which the percussion cap was placed.

SPANISH

The incompatibility of percussion systems introduced in the early nineteenth century led to the development of "dual ignition" weapons. This rare brass-barreled pistol had a firing mechanism that could use both a Forsyth-type priming system and the later percussion cap.

SWISS

This heavy caliber (.70) pistol was made in a Swiss factory in 1855. However, it was assembled largely from French-manufactured parts.

SINGLE-SHOT

A .17 French percussion pistol is a rare early example of the "salon" or "saloon" pistol— a handgun, small both in size and caliber, which could be fired indoors, for personal defense or for target practice.

TWIGG

One of a pair of percussion pistols made by British gunsmith John Twigg, this gun also has a spring dagger mounted below the barrel—a somewhat unusual configuration, as most combination weapons of this type place the blade above the barrel.

GUARDS

This British cavalry pistol, made in 1857, appears to have been carried by a member of the elite Horse Guards regiment. The word "Tower"—for the Royal Armouries at the Tower of London—is stamped on the lock, indicating the weapon passed official inspection.

TURN-OVER

A rare four-barreled turn-over (see p 32) percussion pistol, made by London gunsmith Thomas Lloyd.

LEPAGE

The introduction of the percussion system allowed the development of very small and compact weapons—like the .45 pocket pistol shown here, made by LePage of Paris, one of the leading French gunmakers of the nineteenth century.

EAST INDIA

This percussion holster pistol was made for the British East India Company. Chartered by Queen Elizabeth I in 1600, the company had a monopoly on trade with India and effectively governed Britain's possessions on the subcontinent until 1858. The company had its own army and navy and thus was a major customer for British weapons-makers.

FLINTLOCK TO PERCUSSION CONVERSIONS

It was a fairly easy process to convert a flintlock weapon to the new percussion system; gunsmiths generally had only to replace the flintlock's priming pan with a nipple for the cap and to swap the flint cock with a hammer. As a result, countless flintlock muskets and other firearms were retrofitted as the percussion system grew in popularity. Some interesting and unusual conversions are show here.

SPANISH BLUNDERBUSS

This Spanish blunderbuss (see pp 40–41) was converted from flintlock to percussion; it also has a spring-out dagger mounted above the barrel.

INDIAN

A disadvantage of the percussion system was that the weapon could be fired only as long as the firer had caps. Some gunsmiths got around this by making weapons that used both percussion and flintlock mechanisms. The ingenious Indian rifle shown here has a revolving pan (for priming powder in flintlock mode) and nipple (for caps); the lower part of the flintlock cock doubles as a percussion hammer.

CHINESE

A Chinese gunsmith converted what was originally a matchlock gun (see pp 22–23), probably made in the eighteenth century, into a percussion gun. In this weapon, however, the original matchlock mechanism was modified instead of being totally replaced. The firer had to engage a hook around the back of the hammer, which fell forward to strike the percussion cap when the trigger was squeezed.

DUAL-FIRE PISTOL

Probably made in Switzerland around 1840, this pistol has both flintlock and percussion mechanisms.

BOUTET

A French army officer owned this converted flintlock, originally made by Nicholas Boutet, director of the Arsenal Versailles, at the turn of the nineteenth century.

Pepperboxes and Derringers

Before Samuel Colt's revolvers (see pp 62–65) gained a widespread following in the 1850s, the most popular multiple-shot handgun was the pepperbox pistol. Unlike the revolver, which loads from a cylinder rotating around a single barrel, the pepperbox had multiple rotating barrels—usually four to six. Around the same time, the compact but powerful handguns known as derringers also became popular while gunsmiths around the world developed handguns suited to local requirements, like the "howdah" pistols used in British-ruled India, and the weapons made by indigenous gunsmiths in Darra on what was, in the nineteenth century, the frontier between India and Afghanistan.

THE PEPPERBOX

The pepperbox was the brainchild of Massachusetts gunsmith Ethan Allen (1806–71; apparently no relation to the Revolutionary War hero of the same name), who patented the weapon in 1837 (some sources say 1834) and manufactured it first in Grafton, Massachusetts, then in Norwich, Connecticut, and finally in Worcester, Massachusetts, most of that time in partnership with his brother-in-law under the company name of Allen & Thurber. The weapon is said to have got its name from the fact that the percussion-cap firing system sometimes accidentally discharged all the barrels at once, "peppering" anything (or anyone) in front of it.

The pepperbox was capable of rapid fire, thanks to its double-action firing system (see pp 66–69)—one long pull of the trigger rotated the barrel into position and fired the weapon, and it was immediately ready to fire again with the next trigger pull. Pepperboxes, however, were never renowned for their accuracy. In *Roughing It*, Mark Twain's best-selling account of his Western adventures, the author quotes a stagecoach driver's experience with the weapon: "'If she [the gun] didn't get what she went after, she would fetch something else.' And so she did. She went after a deuce of spades nailed against a tree, once, and fetched a mule standing about thirty yards to the left of it."

The pepperbox fell victim to the growing popularity of the revolver, and Allen & Thurber ceased production of the weapon in the mid-1860s.

THE DERRINGER

"Derringer" is a catch-all term for the small, short-barreled, easily concealable pistols introduced in the 1830s. The name derives from a Philadelphia gunsmith, Henry Deringer (1786–1878). (Generally, firearms historians refer to the weapons made by Deringer himself as "deringers" and those made by his imitators as "derringers.") The original deringers were single-shot, muzzle-loading, percussion-cap weapons, usually .41, and with barrel lengths as short as 1.5in/38mm. Actor John Wilkes Booth used such a weapon to assassinate President Abraham Lincoln at Ford's Theater in Washington, D.C., on the Saturday evening of April 15, 1865.

Later weapons of the type were made by a number of manufacturers, including Colt and Remington; they typically fired cartridges and often had two barrels in an over-and-under configuration. Derringers had widespread appeal as personal-defense weapons because they provided considerable "stopping power"—at least at close range—in a weapon that could be stowed inconspicuously in a coat pocket, or a boot, or tucked into a "lady's" garter belt.

ALLEN & THURBER
A classic Allen & Thurber pepperbox. This six-shot, .36 model was made sometime after 1857. Allen & Thurber guns were famed for their excellent construction; for example, the barrel assembly was machined from a single piece of steel.

MARIETTE
A very finely made Belgian Mariette .38 pepperbox, with a ring trigger, four Damascus-steel barrels, and an ebonized grip. The Mariette system used a key to disengage all four barrels from the frame for loading.

FRENCH
A French pepperbox from around 1840; like the Mariette, it is finely made, and also richly finished with gold and silver inlay.

DARRA
Since the late nineteenth century, the town of Darra Adam Khel (then part of India, now part of Pakistan) has been renowned for its gunsmiths, who are legendary for their ability to produce meticulous copies of the most complex firearms. The gunsmiths of Darra have also made some highly original weapons, like this nineteenth-century pistol chambered to fire 12-gauge shotgun shells.

LADIES CASE WITH PISTOL COMPARTMENT

The derringer's compact size made it a popular personal-defense gun for women—whether "respectable," by nineteenth-century standards, or otherwise. This traveling case, made by Halstaffe of Regent Street, London, has a tray for cosmetics, a hidden compartment for money—and a concealed drawer fitted for two .44, single-shot Colt Model No. 3 derringers. The Model No. 3 was manufactured between 1875 and 1912.

ENGLISH MINIATURES

British gunsmith John Maycock produced this cased set of miniature pepperboxes. The six-shot, 2mm pistols feature 1in/2.5cm blued steel barrels, ivory butts, and brass frames; the mahogany case also holds an ivory cartridge box, ivory-handled screwdriver and cleaning rod, and a brass flask for lubricating oil. These tiny pistols are single-action—i.e., each barrel had to be manually rotated into place—as a double-action mechanism would have been impossible to incorporate into weapons of this diminutive size.

REMINGTON

While perhaps not strictly a derringer, the Remington-Rider magazine pistol, manufactured between 1871 and 1888, meets the derringer criteria of compact size (it had a barrel of 3in/7.6cm), but it fired a special short .32 cartridge. Also, it used an unusual repeating mechanism, with five rounds in a tubular magazine below the barrel. The firer pressed downward on a projection to depress the breechblock, ejecting the spent cartridge and chambering a new one.

HOWDAH

One unusual category of nineteenth-century handguns are the "howdah" pistols used by British officers and colonial officials in India. Howdahs are the passenger-carrying platforms mounted on the backs of elephants, which were a common form of transportation on hunting trips or administrative rounds in rural areas of the Subcontinent. Riders needed a hard-hitting weapon to fend off attacks by tigers, so British gunsmiths produced heavy-caliber pistols (usually .50—like the one shown here—or .60), which were often double-barreled, to give the firer a second shot if the first one missed.

TURN-OVER

A predecessor to the derringer was the turn-over pistol, which had two muzzle-loaded barrels which (as the name implies) could be unscrewed and flipped over, allowing the firer to get off two shots in (relatively) quick succession. The percussion-cap model shown here, made in Britain, features a concealed trigger.

BRITISH DERRINGERS

This pair of .22 double-barreled percussion-cap derringers were made by the firm of Hartwell & Stow.

Colt's Revolvers

While Samuel Colt didn't invent the revolver, his name is now synonymous with the weapon—and for good reasons. First, while the mechanical advances that Colt patented in 1835–36 weren't a huge leap forward in innovation, they collectively made the revolver a practical weapon for both military and civilian use. Second, although it took years for Colt to win widespread acceptance for his revolvers, his skill in marketing the weapon ultimately established the Colt revolver as the standard by which all similar pistols were judged. Finally, Colt's significance to weapon history extends beyond his designs: His factory situated in Hartford, Connecticut, was the first to harness the technical advances of the Industrial Revolution—mass-production using interchangeable parts—and bring them to gunmaking on a large scale.

THE EVOLUTION OF THE REVOLVER

The idea of a repeating firearm that fired successive shots from a cylinder rotating around a single barrel (the opposite of the pepperbox system—see pp 58–59) was not new in the early nineteenth century. Flintlock revolvers were made in England as early as the mid-1600s. The problem with these early revolvers was that each chamber of the cylinder needed its own pan of priming powder, and firing one round sometimes ignited the powder in the rest of the pans, discharging all the cylinders at once.

Around the turn of the nineteenth century an American inventor, Elisha Collier, designed a much improved flintlock revolver that used a single priming pan. A number were manufactured in Britain after around 1810. Despite Collier's advances, it would take the introduction of the percussion cap—and Samuel Colt's basic design, which linked the cylinder to the firing mechanism, eliminating the need to manually rotate the cylinder—to make a truly safe and practical revolver.

Colt's revolvers earned their high reputation because they were powerful, well made, and reliable. That reliability stemmed in large part from their

relative mechanical simplicity. Until the mid-1870s, all Colt models were single-action. To fire, the user pulled back the hammer, which rotated the cylinder and lined up the chamber with the barrel. Then the user had only to pull the trigger to discharge the weapon. This required a mechanism with fewer moving parts than the double-action revolvers (see pp 66–69) developed in the early 1850s. For the

same reason, Colts were also more accurate than their double-action counterparts, if slower to fire. (An experienced user could, however, discharge his Colt quickly by "fanning" the hammer with the palm of his non-shooting hand—a technique familiar from countless Western movies and TV shows.)

PATERSON AND CHARGER

The largest of the first three Colt revolvers—the five-shot .36 "Texas Paterson"—is shown here. Like all revolvers before the introduction of the metallic cartridge, it was a "cap and ball" weapon. Each chamber had to be individually loaded with gunpowder and a bullet (usually known as a ball at the time); a percussion cap was then fitted to a nipple at the rear of the chamber. The Texas Paterson was probably the first revolver to be in used in combat, during one the U.S. Army's several wars against the Seminole Native Americans in Florida in 1835–42.

POCKET

A .31, five-shot, octagon-barrel "Pocket Model" Colt of 1849. According to the inscription engraved on the butt, this particular revolver was presented to a Union officer by "the Ladies of Bristol [Pennsylvania]" in May 1861, shortly after the outbreak of the American Civil War. Its recipient was killed at the Second Battle of Bull Run fifteen months later. The mechanism below the barrel is the compound rammer, which was used to press the ball firmly into each chamber, so the cylinder and barrel formed a tight seal during firing.

NAVY

One of Colt's most successful revolvers was the six-shot .44 "Navy" series, the first model of which appeared in 1851. (Navy Colts weren't specifically made for use at sea; they got their name from the naval scene engraved on their barrels.) As with several other designs, Colt produced a smaller "pocket model," in this case .36. The "Pocket Navy Revolver" shown here was converted from its original percussion-cap firing system to fire .38 centerfire cartridges. (Owners of cap-and-ball Colts could send their pistols back to the Hartford factory for conversion after Colt began making cartridge pistols in the early 1870s.)

"God may have created all men equal, but Sam Colt made them so."

—Popular saying in the "Wild West"

SAMUEL COLT

Born in Hartford, Connecticut, in 1814, Samuel L. Colt was—like most of the great gunmakers—something of a mechanical prodigy: As a boy, he liked to disassemble and reassemble clocks, firearms, and other devices. Bored with working in his father's textile mill, he went to sea at age fifteen as an apprentice seaman. It was on this voyage that he conceived his initial design. The origin of Colt's inspiration is shrouded in legend, variously attributed to his observation of the ship's wheel; or the capstan used to raise the anchor; or a steamboat's paddlewheel—or, more prosaically, he may have seen Collier flintlock revolvers in India, where they were used by British troops. In any event, by the time he returned to the U.S., he had carved a working model out of wood.

To get his gun built, Colt needed money. Billing himself as "Dr. S. Coult," he became a traveling "lecturer" whose specialty was demonstrating the effects of nitrous oxide—laughing gas—on curious locals. With the proceeds he had two gunsmiths, Anton Chase and John Pearson, make experimental models. After receiving his U.S. Patent in 1836, Colt set up the Patent Arms Manufacturing Company in Paterson, New Jersey, to make the new weapon. The three "Paterson" revolver models that appeared that year, however, found few takers. In 1842, Colt went bankrupt. That experience—and the years of litigation that followed—might have driven a lesser personality into despairing retirement. As determined as he was ambitious, Colt made an astonishing comeback a few years later.

Some early Colts had found their way into the hands of soldiers and frontiersmen, including Captain Samuel Walker of the Texas Rangers. In 1844, Walker and fifteen rangers, armed with Colts, fought off a war party of about eighty Comanche Native Americans. When the Mexican-American War broke out in 1846, Walker (now an army officer) and Colt collaborated on a design for a new revolver. The result was the huge (4.9lb/2.2kg), powerful (.41), "Walker Colt." A government order for a thousand put Colt back in business; because he no longer had his own plant, Colt contracted with Eli Whitney Jr. (son of the famous inventor) to make them in Whitneyville, Connecticut.

The success of Colt revolvers in the Mexican-American War greatly raised the weapons' profile, and they began to attract international orders when Colt exhibited his guns at the Great Exhibition in London in 1851 and also when they proved their worth in the Crimean War (1854–55). By 1855, Colt was so successful that he was able to build a huge and highly advanced factory in Hartford, Connecticut—soon to become the world's largest non-government armory.

Colt died in 1862, eleven years before his company's single most successful revolver—the single-action Army Model, and its civilian variants—came into being. Made in several calibers (including 44. and .45), this was the legendary "Peacemaker" and "Six-Shooter" of the American West.

RIFLE

From its beginnings in Paterson, New Jersey, Colt manufactured carbines, rifles, and even shotguns as well as pistols. Most early Colt long arms (such as the Model 1855 .56 carbine shown here) used a revolving cylinder, but later the company made lever- and slide-action (see pp 76–77) guns as well. While Colt's nineteenth-century long arms enjoyed some success in both military and civilian hands, their popularity never reached the level that the company's pistols achieved. At some point in this rifle's history, the barrel was shortened.

NEW NAVY

Introduced in 1892 and produced through 1908, the double-action Colt "New Navy" revolver was typical of the revolvers made by Colt from the late 1880s through the 1910s. (These guns, unlike the earlier "Navy Colts," were actually bought by the U.S. Navy and were the standard sidearm during the Spanish-American War.) Colt revolvers of this era were available in several different barrel lengths and chambered for a range of calibers. The New Navy series was made in .38 and .41—the latter version is shown here.

NEW DOUBLE-ACTION REVOLVER

In the mid-1870s Colt finally began to make double-action pistols, starting with the "Lightning" model. The pistol shown here—which makes use of a slide-rod ejector to push spent cartridges from the cylinder chambers—is a model .38 made for export to Britain.

Colt's Competitors

While Colt's revolvers (see pp 62–65) dominated the field thanks to a combination of patents, marketing, and general excellence, gunmakers on both sides of the Atlantic introduced a number of competing revolver designs, many of which would be combat-tested in battlefields ranging from the Crimea (1854–55) to India (the "mutiny" of 1857), and the United States itself, in the Civil War of 1861–1865 (see pp 70–75), in which an amazing variety of revolvers were used on both sides. The 1850s and 1860s also saw a sort of civil war among gunmakers themselves over real and perceived patent infringement. However, by the 1870s, it was clear that the overall victor (whether double- or single-action) was the cartridge-firing revolver.

DOUBLE VERSUS SINGLE ACTION

At the 1851 Great Exhibition in London—the same "world's fair" at which Samuel Colt proudly displayed his revolvers—British gunsmith Robert Adams (1809–70) exhibited a new type of revolver. Instead of requiring the separate step of cocking the hammer before pulling the trigger, Adams's "double-action" revolver could be cocked and fired with one pull of the trigger. This made it faster to fire than Colt's single-action revolvers, but also less accurate because of the heavy pressure the firer had to exert on the trigger. Early Adams revolvers suffered from various technical problems, but based on combat experience in the Crimean War, an improved version, the Beaumont-Adams, was introduced in 1855.

Revolvers of this type—which could be fired using either single- or double-action—soon became the standard sidearm in the British Army, more or less shutting Colt out of the British market. Although Adams revolvers were purchased for use by both the Union and Confederate armies during the Civil War, Colt retained its dominance in both camps during this era; unlike Colt, which mass-produced its pistols, Adams revolvers were hand-crafted and thus more expensive. The simpler Colt revolvers were also more suited to rugged American conditions, whether on Civil War battlefields or on the plains and deserts of the postwar Western frontier.

THE CARTRIDGE PISTOL

Another potential challenge to Colt came from the introduction of fully enclosed metallic cartridges. In the mid-1850s, Americans Horace Smith and Daniel Wesson (see p 68), who had pioneered both the metallic cartridge and the repeating rifle, developed a revolver firing rimfire cartridges based on a cylinder design purchased from a former Colt employee, Rollin White. (According to some sources, White first offered his design to Samuel Colt, but with an uncharacteristic failure of foresight, Colt didn't think metallic cartridges had any potential.) Smith & Wesson put their pistol, in a .22 model, on the market in 1857, after Colt's patents expired.

The combat advantages of a revolver that could load cartridges quickly—as opposed to the slow-loading cap-and-ball system (see pp 62–65) used by Colt and others—were obvious, and a .32 version proved popular with Union forces during the Civil War. But again, Colt's dominance was not seriously challenged, because S&W's production couldn't keep up with demand, both in pistols and in ammunition. In the last years of the conflict, Colt revolvers did face a serious competitor in the form of the Remington Model 1863 Army revolver. While a cap-and-ball weapon, many soldiers found it to be easier to load and fire than its Colt counterparts. When S&W's patent expired in 1872, Colt and a host of other gunmakers rushed to get cartridge revolvers on the market.

TURRET PISTOL
This very rare and interesting American revolver design appeared around the same time as Samuel Colt's first pistol. Patented by J. W. Cochran of New York City and made by C. B. Allen of Springfield, Massachusetts, the "turret" or "monitor" pistol had a .40, seven-shot, horizontally oriented cylinder. The percussion-cap weapon was fired by a sideways-mounted hammer. Only five or so were made.

COGSWELLL TRANSITION GUN
A major maker of pepperbox pistols (see pp 58–59), the London gunmakers Cogswell & Harrison also produced this revolver—known to firearms historians as a "transition gun"—in the early 1850s. The single-action weapon had a six-shot cylinder firing .44 rounds.

MASSACHUSETTS ARMS CASED SET
Between about 1849 and 1851, Massachusetts Arms also made Wesson & Leavitt revolvers, like the .31, six-shot model one shown here cased with its accessories.

MASSACHUSETTS ARMS COMPANY .28
In 1851, Colt sued the Massachusetts Arms Company of Chicopee Falls, Massachusetts, for patent infringement. The Massachusetts Company claimed that its revolvers—which used a bevel-gear system to rotate the cylinder, rather than the pawl-and-ratchet system used by Colt—were significantly different than Colt's, but the court eventually ruled in favor of Colt. The Massachusetts Arms Company, however, stayed in business and produced some popular pistols, like the .28 six-shot revolver shown here, which was unusual in that it could use either single percussion caps or the Maynard tape-primer system.

SMITH & WESSON

Horace Smith (b. Cheshire, Massachusetts; 1808–93) and Daniel Wesson (b. Worcester, Massachusetts; 1825–96) both entered the gunmaking trade in their youth: Smith as an employee of the federal armory at Springfield, Massachusetts, and Wesson as an apprentice to his elder brother Edwin, a leading New England gunsmith. The two first joined forces in Norwich, Connecticut, in the early 1850s, when they collaborated to produce a repeating rifle that could fire metallic cartridges. As with Samuel Colt, their technological innovation didn't meet with commercial success at first, and they had to sell out to Oliver Winchester (see p 77). But also like Colt, they persevered, patenting a revolver firing a rimfire cartridge (1854) and reconstituting their company (1856). The success of their designs during the Civil War and in the years that followed—especially the Model 3 revolver, introduced in 1870—laid the foundations of a company that remains one of the foremost gunmakers in the twenty-first century. While Smith & Wesson today manufacture automatics, revolvers continue to be the firm's signature product, and long after the death of its founders, their tradition of innovation continued in such weapons as the .38 Model 1910 "Military & Police" revolver (introduced in 1899 and still in production through numerous variations, and probably the most popular pistol ever made for law-enforcement use); the .357 (1935) and .44 (1956) magnums (beloved by Hollywood—Clint Eastwood's character "Dirty Harry" wielded the latter); and the Model 60 (1965), which ushered in the era of the stainless steel pistol.

SLOCUM
In 1863, the Brooklyn Arms Company of New York introduced a .32 five-shot revolver, the "Slocum," named apparently for a New York–born Civil War general. The pistol loaded from the front; the chambers were actually sliding tubes that moved forward over a fixed ejecting mechanism.

REMINGTON NEW ARMY
The .44 six-shot "New Army" revolver was (after the Colt Model 1860) perhaps the second most widely issued revolver for Union troops during the American Civil War (1861–65; see pp 70–71). At least 130,000 were manufactured at Remington's Ilion, New York, factory.

SMITH & WESSON

The six-shot, .32 Smith & Wesson No. 2 revolver,
which saw much use in the Civil War and on the Western frontier, was—like
other early Smith & Wessons—known as a "tip-up" revolver from the system
it used for loading and extracting cartridges: Manipulating a catch released the barrel to swing
upward, allowing the cylinder to be removed completely from the frame; the firer used the spike
below the barrel to push out the spent cartridges; the cylinder was then reloaded, replaced, and
the barrel swung downward into firing position. Later Smith & Wesson revolvers pioneered the
"break-open" system, in which the barrel swung downward and an extractor mechanism in the
cylinder (which remained attached to the frame) ejected all the spent cartridges at once.

TRANTER

Based in Birmingham, England, British gunsmith William Tranter
(1816–1890) produced a variety of revolver designs in his long
career; his pistols had a high reputation for quality, and large
numbers were purchased by the Confederate government for
issue to its forces in the American Civil War (1861–65), while
others (like the five-shot .54 pistol shown here) were bought
privately by British officers. This model used a double-trigger
firing system; the lower trigger cocked the weapon, the upper
one fired it. It's a cap-and-ball pistol, but after the Civil War,
Tranter produced many cartridge-firing designs.

ALLEN & WHEELOCK

Another interesting early cartridge pistol was the .32 "lipfire" revolver
made by the Allen & Wheelock Company of Worcester, Massachusetts.
First made in 1858, these pistols not only fired a unique cartridge, but
also utilized a lever-operated, rack-and-pinion ejection system.

MOORE

In an effort to get around Smith & Wesson's patent on cartridge
revolvers, Moore's Patent Firearms Company of Brooklyn made a number
of revolvers based on a design by Daniel Moore and Daniel Wilson in the
1860s. Instead of loading from the rear of the cylinder, these revolvers
loaded from the front; the cartridge's priming charge was contained in a
"teat" in its base, and so these revolvers became known as "teat," or
"tit," guns. The courts eventually found for Smith & Wesson.

The American Civil War

The American Civil War (1861–65) is often described, with much justification, as the first modern war. The conflict saw the introduction (or at least the first widespread use) of innovations like photography, the telegraph, aircraft (balloons, used for observation of enemy forces), submarines, armored ships, breech-loading artillery, and infantry weapons, repeating rifles, and rapid-fire guns. Almost a century and a half later, the Civil War remains both the greatest war fought in the Western Hemisphere and America's deadliest conflict, with a combined death toll estimated at 700,000—more than in all other American wars combined. While disease claimed twice as many men as combat, the high casualty rate owed much to technical advances in weaponry.

TACTICS AND TECHNOLOGY

The Civil War was a classic example of technology outstripping tactics. At the beginning, commanders on both sides envisioned that the war would be fought in the traditional style—by masses of men maneuvering in the open in stand-up combat, with infantry exchanging volleys and charging the opposing line with the bayonet, with artillery in support and cavalry waiting to exploit any breakthrough.

These tactics worked in the eighteenth century and the Napoleonic Wars (see pp 48–51), when armies fought with smoothbore muskets that were inaccurate at all but the closest ranges. The years before the Civil War, however, saw a revolution in infantry weapons. The old smoothbore musket had given way to the rifle (or rifled musket, as it was also known), which was the standard infantryman's weapon on both sides. These fired a heavy lead bullet (usually .58 caliber) to an effective range of up to 500yd/0.45 kilometer. While still muzzle-loaders, these rifles used a new type of bullet, the Minié ball (named for French army officer, Claude Minié, who invented it in 1847). The Minié ball expanded upon firing to snugly fit the grooves of a rifled barrel, greatly increasing accuracy.

The result of these innovations, when translated into impact on human flesh, was horrifying. If not killed outright, a Civil War soldier hit in the abdomen would likely die of infection, given the crude medical treatment of the era. If hit in a limb, amputation was the usual outcome. Head shots were generally immediately fatal.

The introduction of the rifle shifted the advantage from the offensive to the defensive on the battlefield. Riflemen "dug in" to the ground or otherwise behind cover, firing several shots a minute, could easily mow down several times their number attacking in the open.

Confederate commanders, especially Robert E. Lee, were quicker to grasp that the rules of warfare had changed than their Union counterparts. However, even Lee made the mistake of sending infantry across open ground against fixed positions in the Battle of Malvern Hill (July 1, 1862) during the Peninsular Campaign and again a year later in "Pickett's Charge" during the Battle of Gettysburg—the latter a miscalculation that probably doomed the Confederacy to ultimate defeat.

EXPERIMENTATION AND INNOVATION

The Civil War also saw the introduction of weapons that were "high-tech" for their time. Because it was virtually impossible to use a muzzle-loading weapon in the saddle, Union cavalry rode into battle armed with breech-loading weapons like the Burnside and Sharps (see p 78) carbines. Especially effective was the repeating Spencer carbine, which had a seven-shot magazine—Confederate soldiers called it "That damned Yankee gun that can be loaded on Sunday and fired all week." Because the Confederacy was largely unable to manufacture similar weapons, captured breech-loaders and repeaters were prized by Southern soldiers.

Both sides also raised units of marksmen to engage in what would later become known as sniping. The best-known of these units was the Union army's Berdan's Sharpshooters, commanded by Hiram Berdan (1823–1893), who was already famous as a civilian target-shooting champion. (The term "sharpshooters" may derive from their use of Sharps breech-loading rifles. Confederate snipers tended to use the British-designed Whitworth rifle.)

While the technology of the time was not sufficient to permit the development of machine guns in the modern sense, both sides experimented with manually operated rapid-fire weapons. The Confederacy apparently used a crank-operated light cannon during the Peninsular Campaign, and the Union deployed a multiple-barreled bullet-firing weapon, the Requa-Billnghurst battery gun, mainly to defend bridges and other positions. The best-known of these weapons is the Gatling gun (see p 73), although it only saw limited service very late in the war.

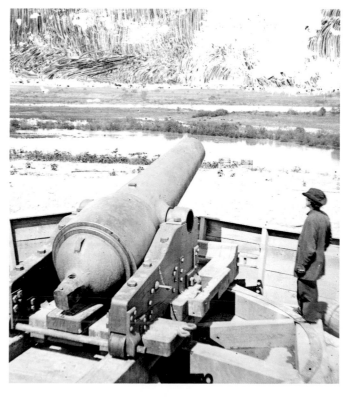

Union Weapons of the American Civil War

In terms of weapons production, the Union was much more fortunate than the Confederacy (see pp 74–75); the northern states contained not only most government arsenals, but the region was also much more heavily industrialized than the South. Although the Union, like the Confederacy, had to scramble for weapons to equip its troops early in the war, by 1862 the Union had largely settled on a few standardized firearms whose manufacture could be contracted out to private firms. By 1864, the Union was self-sufficient in weapons production, while the Confederacy still relied on imports for many of its firearms.

THE SPRINGFIELD RIFLED MUSKET
The closest thing to a standard Union infantry long arm was the Springfield rifled musket. The weapon got its name from the federal government's arsenal at Springfield, Massachusetts, which had been founded in 1794, and where many were manufactured—although during the war, more than thirty companies produced Springfields under contract, for a total of about 1.5 million pieces.

-ggThe most common version of the weapon was the Model 1861, but the first of the .58 Springfield series appeared in the 1840s, when the U.S. Army began to replace .69 flintlock muskets with percussion-cap weapons, which after 1855 incorporated a rifled barrel as well. The greater accuracy of the rifle over its smoothbore predecessors also led to the introduction of a ladder-style rear sight, and it came with a spike bayonet. It was a heavy piece, weighing in at 9.25lb/4.2kg, with an overall length of about 58in/147cm—which meant that with bayonet fixed, the Springfield was about as tall as the average Civil War soldier.

Springfields were also widely used by the Confederacy—some were seized when the federal arsenal at Harper's Ferry, Virginia, fell to Stonewall Jackson's troops during the campaign that culminated in the Battle of Antietam (September 1862), and many others were obtained by battlefield scavenging.

CARBINES AND PISTOLS
The Union was also fortunate in being able to take advantage of the designs of gunmakers like Christian Sharps, Christopher Spencer, and Benjamin Tyler Henry, who produced innovative breech-loading (and, in the case of Spencer and Henry, repeating) rifles and carbines. However, these weapons were never issued in large numbers by the Union's Ordnance Department; many of them were purchased by state governments for issue to their regiments, or were personally bought by individual soldiers. In the opinion of some historians, the Union might have defeated the Confederacy more quickly had it been less conservative in adopting these kinds of weapons.

As for the Union Army's pistols, these, too were a mix of government-issue and privately purchased weapons. The .44 Colt Model 1860 was probably the most popular single revolver among Union officers, but a wide variety of revolvers were used, including the Starr (also .44), British-made Adams revolvers, and the .36 Savage-North "Navy" model shown below.

SAVAGE-NORTH REVOLVER
Manufactured by the Savage Revolving Arms Co. of Middletown, Connecticut, the 1859 "Navy Model" revolver—a six-shot, .36 weapon—had an unusual firing system. The trigger guard enclosed not one but two triggers: The lower ring trigger rotated the cylinder and cocked the hammer, while the conventional upper trigger fired it. Despite its designation as a "Navy" revolver, the Union Navy apparently purchased only about a thousand, while the Union Army bought ten times that number.

SPRINGFIELD MUSKET

In the first year or so of the war, many Union troops were issued with a version of the old .69 flintlock musket converted to the percussion-cap firing system, like the gun shown here, though this one has been cut down to two bands from the usual three. The Springfield rifled musket would largely replace these obsolete weapons over time, although many of the conversions remained in service with state militias.

SPENCER CARBINE

The Spencer rifle, model 1860, has the distinction of being the first magazine-fed repeating rifle officially adopted by a major army. The gun, designed by Christopher Spencer (1833–1922), utilized a falling-block breech, operated by a lever that doubled as a trigger, fed by a tubular magazine of seven .56 copper-jacketed cartridges located in the stock. After the war started, both the Union army and navy placed orders for the weapon, but Spencer's company had an impossible delivery deadline, and unfortunate accidents in testing led the government to have second thoughts. Spencer personally called on President Abraham Lincoln in August 1863, and the president test-fired the weapon to his satisfaction. The Union ultimately bought more than 100,000 Spencers, including the carbine model shown here.

GATLING GUN

The original Gatling gun of 1861 had six barrels and fed from a hopper containing paper cartridges; a later model took metallic cartridges, greatly increasing the rate of fire, and post–Civil War models—like the one shown here—had ten barrels and utilized a drum magazine. The Gatling is often cited as the world's first machine gun, but this is an inaccurate description, as the weapon was manually operated, rather than functioning by means of recoil or gas energy. Still, Gatlings could achieve a rate of fire in excess of 1,000 rounds per minute.

RICHARD GATLING

Ironically, Richard Jordan Gatling (1818–1903), the inventor of the Gatling gun—which first saw action with the Union Army in the siege of Petersburg, Virginia, in 1864—was a North Carolinian by birth and (according to some historians) a Confederate sympathizer. In another irony, Gatling (a doctor by training) claimed that his inspiration in developing the weapon—considered to be the first successful rapid-fire gun—was the desire to lower the number of men needed to fight battles in order to reduce the spread of disease: "It occurred to me that if I could invent a machine—a gun—which could by its rapidity of fire, enable one man to do as much battle duty as a hundred, that it would, to a large extent supersede the necessity of large armies, and consequently, exposure to battle and disease [would] be greatly diminished." In 1861, Gatling designed a multiple-barreled, hand-cranked weapon, which he demonstrated to the U.S. Ordnance Bureau a year later. The weapon was rejected in 1862 as too complicated and heavy, and it was not officially adopted until 1866, after the war's end—but, as per above, some commanders purchased Gatlings on their own initiative and these saw service toward the end of the conflict. In later decades, Britain's Royal Navy adopted guns based on the Gatling design, and Gatlings were used to good effect by the U.S. Army in Cuba during the Spanish-American War (1898). After World War II, the multiple-barrel Gatling concept was revived by the U.S. military—in an electrically operated form—in aircraft weapons like the M1961 Vulcan 20mm cannon and the 7.62mm "minigun" machine gun.

Confederate Weapons of the American Civil War

Both "Johnny Reb" and "Billy Yank," the ordinary infantrymen of the American Civil War (1861–65), carried essentially the same weapon—a muzzle-loading rifled musket, usually .58 or .577 caliber. While the workshops and factories of the North kept the Union armies relatively well supplied with weapons (despite shortages early in the war), the South lacked industry and had to import most of its arms from Europe, something that became increasingly difficult as the war went on and the Union Navy's blockade of Southern ports cut the Confederacy off from its sources of supply.

STARTING FROM SCRATCH

Early in the war, the severe Southern arms shortage forced many Confederate soldiers to arm themselves with shotguns and hunting rifles from home.

Contemporary historian Andrew Leckie writes that "When the 27th Alabama [Regiment] marched off to war it was said the men carried a thousand double-barreled shotguns and a thousand homemade Bowie knives." The situation improved somewhat when arms began arriving from overseas, and when Confederate forces captured the federal arsenal at Harper's Ferry, Virginia, in 1861. Some of the machinery from Harper's Ferry was used to set up arms factories throughout the South, but these small manufacturers could produce only a fraction of the rifles, artillery pieces, and other weapons needed by the Confederacy.

IMPORTS AND IMITATIONS

The closest thing to a standard infantry weapon in the Confederate armies was the British-made .577 Enfield rifled musket. Despite the name, the Enfields used in the Civil War were not in fact made at the Royal Arsenal at Enfield, England, because Great Britain was officially neutral in the conflict; instead, private manufacturers produced rifles to

JEFFERSON DAVIS

Unlike Abraham Lincoln—whose only military experience was a brief stint in the Illinois militia—Jefferson Davis spent many years as a professional soldier before assuming the presidency of the Confederate States of America in February 1861. Born in Kentucky in 1808, Davis graduated from West Point and saw service on the frontier before resigning his commission in 1835. He later fought with distinction—and was wounded—in the Mexican-American War (1846–48). Entering politics as Secretary of War in President Franklin Pierce's cabinet, he pushed through significant reforms like the adoption of the rifled musket. Davis was a U.S. Senator from Mississippi when the war broke out. Imprisoned for two years after the Confederacy defeat in the spring of 1865, he died in Louisiana in 1889.

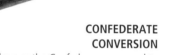

CONFEDERATE CONVERSION

Early in the war the Confederacy managed to obtain a small quantity of converted muzzle-loaders made by the Massachusetts Arms Company, like the one shown here. The carbine used the Maynard Percussion Tape Primer system, rather than the more common percussion cap.

the Enfield pattern for export. The Confederate government purchased about 400,000 Enfields over the course of the war, and the rifle was also widely used by Union forces. Besides the Enfield, the Confederacy bought around 50,000 Model 1854 Infanteriegewehr (infantry rifles) from Austria.

Throughout the war, the Confederate cavalry lacked an effective breech-loading saddle weapon like the Sharps carbine (see p 78) used by Union horsemen. Confederate gunsmiths tried to copy the Sharps, but the result—the so-called "Richmond Sharps," named for the Confederate capital, where it was manufactured—performed so poorly that Confederate General Robert E. Lee described the gun as "so defective as to be demoralizing to our men." Only about 5,000 were made.

BELGIAN REVOLVER
Made in Belgium in the mid-nineteenth century, this early six-shot revolver is .38 caliber with a pinfire mechanism.

LEMAT PISTOL
A favorite sidearm of Confederate officers, the LeMat pistol had two barrels: The upper discharged .40 bullets via a nine-shot cylinder, the lower a single charge of buckshot. This powerful hybrid of revolver and shotgun was first made in New Orleans in 1856 by a French-born doctor, Jean Alexander Francois LeMat, who later moved production to Europe when the war broke out.

JEFFERSON DAVIS' PISTOLS
This magnificent set of cased pistols was made in Belgium in 1861 for presentation to the newly appointed president of the Confederate States of America. They feature Damascus steel barrels, grips of fluted, carved ivory, and gold inlay on the frames and other parts. Davis never got to enjoy this gift, however; the ship carrying them to the Confederacy was captured as it tried to run the Union blockade.

AUSTRIAN STEEL
This socket bayonet fit the Model 1854 Austrian Infanteriegewehr, also known as the Lorenz rifled musket. Despite being purchased in large numbers by both sides, the Lorenz, according to one historian, was "universally loathed by many of the soldiers who used them." In fact, the Union government bought thousands of these guns simply to keep them from being bought by the Confederacy.

Weapons of the American West

Few eras in history are more identified with the widespread use of firearms than the settling of western United States in the nineteenth century: The phrase "Wild West" instantly conjures up images of cowboys, outlaws, and lawmen wielding "six-shooters"; scouts and buffalo-hunters with their lever-action "repeaters" and high-powered single-shot rifles; Cavalrymen and Native Americans skirmishing with carbines and revolvers pitted against arrows and lances. Countless books and movies have established this romantic period in the popular imagination—not always accurately—but the fact is that on the frontier, having a reliable gun (or two, or three) to hand often meant the difference between life and death.

ACROSS THE MOUNTAINS

At the start of the nineteenth century, the frontier was just over the Appalachian Mountains; westward-moving pioneers from the states of the Eastern Seaboard brought with them their long Kentucky rifles both to bag game for the pot and to fight the Native Americans who resisted the tide of settlement. When the Louisiana Purchase (1803) pushed the frontier to the Rocky Mountains and beyond, the legendary "Mountain Men" went into the wilderness in search of furs, often armed with the heavy caliber rifles manufactured by the brothers Samuel and Jacob Hawken of St. Louis.

In the 1850s, during the run-up to the American Civil War the western territory of Kansas became a battleground as antislavery settlers from the North clashed with proslavery settlers from the South, each side hoping to gain a majority when the time came for the territory to apply for statehood. Many of the Northern settlers were armed with a new and technically advanced weapon—the carbine designed by Christian Sharps (1811–74) in 1848. The breech-loading Sharps had a falling-block action; a lever (which doubled as the trigger guard) dropped the breechblock for loading. Rifles and carbines based on the Sharps design remained popular in the West for decades.

ON THE FRONTIER

The original Sharps was a single-shot weapon, but in 1860 Christopher Spencer (1833-1922) introduced a falling-block rifle with a tubular seven-round magazine under the barrel—a true "repeater"—which also saw widespread use in the West. Around the same time, the Winchester Repeating Arms Co. was developing a lever-action magazine rifle, which it introduced in 1866; its successor, the Model 1873, proved immensely popular and has often been called "the gun that won the West."

The U.S. Army's main task from the end of the Civil War until the "end of the frontier" in 1890 was fighting the Native Americans. Although repeaters had proved their worth in the Civil War, the army had so many Springfield muzzle-loaders left over from that conflict that they fought the Indian Wars largely with "trap-door" Springfields—so-called because they'd been converted to single-shot breech-loaders.

Another category of Western weapon was the high-powered (usually .50 caliber) rifles used by professional buffalo hunters. Killed for their hides, to keep them from blocking railroad construction, or just for sport, the buffalo—whose herds had once ranged across the Western plains in hundreds of thousands—were nearly extinct by the mid-1880s.

As for pistols, those on either side of the law used a wide variety, but Colts—especially the 1873 single-action Army model—were favorites.

WINCHESTER 66

The Winchester Model 1866 was nicknamed "the Yellow Boy," because of the color of its receiver. A direct descendant of the Henry rifle, the gun fired the same .44 rimfire cartridge, but its tubular magazine more than doubled the Henry's capacity, from seven to fifteen rounds. This particular model (converted to centerfire) was owned by Czar Alexander II of Russia (1818–81) and is engraved with the czar's royal cipher and other symbols of the Russian monarchy.

OLIVER WINCHESTER

Born in Boston in 1810, Oliver Fisher Winchester made his first fortune as a manufacturer of men's shirts in Baltimore, New York City, and New Haven. As his clothing business prospered, he invested in the Volcanic Repeating Arms Company, taking control of that firm in 1856 and renaming it the New Haven Arms Co., and, later, the Winchester Repeating Arms Co. The Volcanic Company had produced a briefly popular repeating rifle, and Winchester hired gunsmith Benjamin Tyler Henry (1821–98) to refine the design. The result, in 1860, was the so-called Henry rifle, a lever-action repeater, which saw service in the American Civil War (1861–65; see pp 70–75), even though the Union Army never officially adopted it. After the war Winchester introduced the Model 1866, the Model 1873, and their successors. Winchester was also a politician, serving as lieutenant governor of Connecticut (1866–67). Oliver Winchester died in 1881 and control of the company passed to his son, William Winchester. William died the following year, but the company went on, and it remains one of the great American armsmakers, producing a wide range of rifles and shotguns for the sporting market. In a curious footnote to the Winchester story, William's widow, Sarah Pardee Winchester, was supposedly told by a Spiritualist medium that she had to build a home for the souls of those killed by Winchester weapons, or else the family would be forever cursed. Whether this is true or not is still debated, but in 1884 Sarah moved to San Jose, California, where she bought a modest house, which she proceeded to expand, at enormous cost, until her death in 1922. By that time the dwelling had 160 rooms and a host of bizarre features like staircases that went nowhere and doors that opened onto walls. The Winchester "mystery house" is now a major tourist attraction.

COLT LIGHTNING RIFLE

In the early 1880s Colt introduced its "Lightning" series of rifles, based on a patent by William Elliott. Unusual for the time, the rifles used a pump, or slide, action, and they were never as popular as the lever-action guns of competitors like Winchester. The several models of the series were chambered for .32, .38, and .44.

MASSACHUSETTS ARMS COMPANY CARBINE

A breech-loading percussion .50 caliber carbine made by the Massachusetts Arms Company; this type of rifle, accurate up to 600, was known as a Maynard Carbine because it used Maynard primer tape for igniting the powder. The carbine was popular with the military as well as sportsmen. It was patented in 1851 and later saw wide use in the Confederate Army during the Civil War. However, this particular rifle, with its silver cartouche and the Napoleonic emblem, was actually owned by Napoleon III (1808–73; r. 1852–70), Napoleon Bonaparte's nephew.

WINCHESTER M1866 MAXIMILIAN RIFLE

This Model 1866 rifle was created by the Winchester Arms Company as a gift to Spanish-appointed Mexican ruler Emperor Maximilian. Maximilian's weapon has a solid ivory stock, gold-plated lock mechanism, and is engraved with the Mexican eagle.

WINCHESTER 73

In 1873 Winchester produced an improved version of the Model 1866 chambered for a new, centerfire version of the .44 round. The "Winchester '73" became the most famous of the Winchester rifles and one of the most celebrated guns of the West, period. The gun shown here was owned by Albert Edward, Prince of Wales, later King Edward VII (1841–1910); the silver medallion inset into the stock is engraved with imperial symbols including the Star of India. The rifle received a special blued vision by the gunsmith James Kerr at the London Armoury Co.

SHARPS 1859

The rolling-block carbines and rifles designed by Christian Sharps (1811–74) were popular with hunters, scouts, and other Western denizens. Shown here is the 1859 Sharps New Model carbine, with a pair of colored "sharpshooter's glasses" used to cut down on glare. Perhaps the most famous Sharps model was the .50 rifle—known as the "Big Fifty"—which was widely used by buffalo hunters. The weapon could reportedly drop a buffalo at 200yd/183m with a single shot.

WILLIAMS & POWELL REVOLVER

This is a five-shot, double-action revolver, made by Williams and Powell of Liverpool, England in the late-nineteenth century.

ADAMS REVOLVER

The revolvers made by the British gunsmith Robert Adams (1809–70) were a serious competitor to Colt's products both during the Civil War and on the Western frontier. As double-action revolvers, they were faster firing, but Colts were generally more accurate and powerful. The finely crafted Adams pistols were also more expensive. Colonel George Armstrong Custer of the U.S. Seventh Cavalry, which was famously wiped out by Sioux and Cheyenne warriors at the Battle of the Little Bighorn in 1876, is said to have carried an Adams pistol similar to the one shown here—although in that fateful battle Custer apparently went to his death firing a pair of Schofield revolvers.

ELIPHALET REMINGTON

Born in Connecticut in 1793, Eliphalet Remington moved—like many New Englanders of the time—to upstate New York, where he worked as a blacksmith alongside his father. In his early twenties, he decided that he could make a better gun than those available for commercial purchase. The resulting weapon impressed local users so much that he entered into gunmaking full-time, establishing what would become E. Remington & Sons (later the Remington Arms Co.) in Ilion, New York. By the time Remington died in 1861, the small firm was on its way to becoming one of the nation's leading gunmakers—a status that, like Winchester, it retains today. Although Remington diversified to produce products ranging from typewriters to bicycles, it's said that the Remington Arms Co. is the oldest American company still making its original product.

BELLE STAR REVOLVER

The famous female outlaw Belle Star (1848–89) carried this five-shot, .36, single-action "Navy Model" revolver, which was manufactured by the Manhattan Firearms Co. of Newark, New Jersey, between 1859 and 1868. Known in her time as "the female Jesse James," Starr is said to have liked to ride through the streets of Western towns firing her revolver in the air. After a career that included a stint in prison for horse theft (and the violent deaths of most of the men in her life) Starr herself was killed by a shotgun blast in Eufaula, Oklahoma.

REMINGTON RIFLE

The single-shot, rolling-block Remington rifles of the 1860s and 1870s were of extremely rugged construction. In America they remained mainly a civilian weapon, although the U.S. Army and Navy purchased some rifles and carbines in small numbers. Remington, however, sold hundreds of thousands of the weapons to foreign governments—some of which remained in service well into the twentieth century.

CUSTER'S LAST STAND

Bolt-Action Magazine Rifles

The bolt-action, magazine-fed rifle, firing a completely enclosed metallic cartridge of substantial caliber and firepower, was the principal infantry weapon of modern armies for about seventy-five years, from the 1860s until the World War II era, when it was replaced by self-loading rifles (see pp 110–13) and later by selective-fire assault rifles (see pp 140–43). Simple, robust, and reliable, this type of rifle continues in use into the twenty-first century among civilians for hunting and target shooting.

NEEDLE-GUN AND CHASSEPOT

While the American Civil War (1861–65; see pp 70–75) demonstrated the effectiveness of rapid-fire, breech-loading rifles and carbines, the powerful German state of Prussia had already adopted such a weapon for its army in 1848. This was the so-called "needle gun" developed by Nikolaus von Dreyse (1787–1867). The 15.4mm gun got its name because it used a needle-shaped firing pin to explode a primer cap embedded in a paper cartridge that also comprised the main powder charge and bullet.

The needle gun's great innovation, besides the incorporation of a self-contained cartridge, was the introduction of a bolt-handle firing mechanism. Together, these advances made for faster loading and firing than was possible with the muzzle-loading, percussion-cap muskets and rifles in use at the time. The weapon's chief disadvantages were that the explosion of the primer cap tended to weaken and eventually corrode the needle firing pin, and the design of the breech, which allowed much propellant gas to escape in firing.

The needle gun first saw action against revolutionary mobs in 1848–49 and then in Prussia's wars against Denmark (1864), Austria (1866), and France (1870–71). In the Franco-Prussian War, Prussian troops with needle guns faced French infantry armed with a similar weapon, the chassepot, named for its inventor, Antoine Chassepot (1833–1905), which the French Army had adopted in 1866. The 11mm chassepot was technically superior to the needle gun in several respects and had a longer range, but Prussian superiority in artillery and tactics countered its advantages.

ENTER THE MAGAZINE

The success of the needle gun and the chassepot led to the adoption of the bolt-action rifles by other Western armies. The needle gun and chassepot, however, were single-shot weapons; the next step forward was the development of multiple-shot magazine weapons utilizing the new firing system. In 1868, for example, the Swiss Army adopted a rifle developed by Freidrich Vetterli (1822–82), which fed from a tubular magazine under the barrel.

Most of this new generation of rifles, though, used a fixed or detachable box magazine holding five or more cartridges, charged either with individual rounds or by means of a stripper clip, which held several cartridges in a metal frame and which was inserted into the magazine from either the top or bottom.

The British Army adopted its first magazine bolt-action rifle, the Lee-Metford, in 1877. In 1889, Denmark adopted the Krag-Jorgensen, which was later adopted by Norway and the United States. The most successful of the new-style rifles, however, were the designs produced by the German brothers Wilhelm and Paul Mauser (see feature).

BELGIAN POLICE CARBINE
This Belgian police carbine is a percussion-cap weapon manufactured in 1858.

THE MAUSERS

Wilhelm (1834–1882) and Paul Mauser (1838–1914) followed in their father's footsteps as gunsmiths at the royal armory in the German kingdom of Wurttemberg. When the government of the newly unified Germany sought an improved rifle in response to the performance of the French chassepot in the Franco-Prussian War, the brothers developed a single-shot bolt-action weapon, the Gewehr (rifle) Model 1871, which Germany adopted that same year.

After Wilhelm's death, Paul came up with a new 7mm design based on the newly developed box magazine. In Models 1893, 1894, and 1895, the rifle proved hugely successful and orders poured in from around the world. While the Mauser's straight-pull bolt didn't allow for as rapid a rate of fire as, say, the British SMLE, it was strong, safe, and effective. In 1898 Mauser introduced the 7.92mm Gewehr 98—the finest bolt-action rifle ever made, in the opinion of many weapons historians. The G98 remained in

service with the Germany Army until the mid-1930s, when it was replaced by a shorter version, the Karabiner (KAR) 98. The three principal Mauser factories were destroyed during World War II; today, the company—now owned by Rheinmetall—makes mostly hunting rifles. Several former Mauser engineers, however, were instrumental in founding Heckler & Koch, Germany's greatest weapons-maker of the post–World War II era.

KRAG

Developed in the 1880s by two Norwegians, Army officer Ole Krag and gun designer Erik Jorgensen, the Krag-Jorgensen rifle was unusual in that it a side-mounted "capsule" five-round magazine. The Krag-Jorgensen went through a variety of models and calibers in Danish and Norwegian service. The U.S. Army adopted it, in "30-40 Krag" caliber, in 1892, although few reached troops until later in the decade. The superior performance of the Mausers used by Spanish forces in Cuba during the Spanish-American War (1898), however, would eventually lead the U.S. to adopt a Mauser-type rifle, the Springfield Model 1903, five years later. In the meantime, the Krag was also widely used by American forces in the Philippines during the pro-independence "insurrection" that followed the U.S. seizure of the islands from Spain.

BELGIAN CARBINE

Firing a .45 centerfire cartridge, this single-shot, breech-loading Belgian carbine is typical of the cavalry weapons developed in the 1860s and 1870s. Following the introduction of bolt-action magazine rifles, weapons designers sought to "split the difference" between carbines and infantry rifles with general purpose weapons like the British SMLE (Short Magazine Lee Enfield) and the U.S. Springfield Model 1903.

BEAUMONT "MOUSQUETON"

In the early 1870s, a Dutch engineer named Beaumont developed a turnbolt-action, single-shot rifle based on the French chassepot. The rifle was unusual in that its action used a V-spring placed inside a hollow, two-piece bolt handle, rather than the coil mainspring found in other bolt-action rifles. This particular model, an experimental carbine for use by artilleryman, was made at the French arsenal at St. Etienne in 1874.

"TORINO"

In 1887, the Italian Army began retrofitting an 1870 Vetterli single-shot bolt-action rifle design with a box magazine designed by artillery officer G. Vitali. The result, a 10.4mm Vetterli-Vitali, saw much service in Italy's colonial wars in Africa during the late nineteenth and early twentieth centuries.

GEWEHR 1888

Afraid of falling behind the French in rifle development, the German Army set up a commission in 1888 to spur innovation. One result was the Gewehr Model 1888, aka the 7.92mm "commission rifle," which incorporated elements from both Mauser and Austrian Mannlicher designs. One unusual feature was that a metal sleeve, rather than the usual wooden forestock, surrounded the barrel: It was thought that this would be a more effective means of keeping the barrel from overheating during rapid fire.

SMLE

During the Boer War (1899–1902) the British Army decided that modern combat conditions demanded a shorter infantry rifle that could double as a carbine, greatly reducing the logistical hassles of supplying two types of parts and ammunition. The result, introduced in 1907, was the .303 SMLE (Short Magazine Lee Enfield), which would remain in service, in various models, for more almost a half-century. Shown here is the Mark III model, with its 18in/46cm sword-type bayonet. The SMLE had a magazine capacity of ten rounds, at a time when most other magazine rifles held five rounds.

MOSIN

Few service rifles have had a longer active life than the Russian 7.62mm Model 1891 Mosin-Nagant; with variations, it served with Russian and Soviet forces through the late 1940s. Prior to the Russian Revolution, many Mosin-Nagants were manufactured in the U.S., including this one, shown with its spike bayonet, which was made by the Westinghouse Corporation in the 1890s.

VETTERLI

Preceding the more famous Mauser by several years, Switzerland's .41 Model 1869 Vetterli infantry rifle was the first multiple-shot, bolt-action rifle adopted by a major army—though it fed from a twelve-round tubular magazine, in a manner similar to the Winchester and Henry rifles, rather than from a box magazine. The model shown here is an Italian version from 1878.

A MULTITUDE OF MAUSERS

Scores of nations adopted Mauser designs for their armed forces; according to the company, some 100 million Mauser rifles were manufactured worldwide from the late nineteenth-century through World War II. Shown here are just a few of the many Mauser variants from across the globe.

TURKISH MAUSER
A Turkish model from 1890, chambered for a slightly different version of the standard 7.65 round.

PERSIAN MAUSER
An 8mm Persian (later Iranian) Army Mauser with bayonet. Many of these were manufactured at the Brno Arms Works in Czechoslovakia.

ARGENTINE MAUSER
ARGENTINE MAUSER BAYONET AND SCABBARD
In 1891, Argentina's army replaced its antiquated .43 Remington rolling-block action rifle with the 7.55mm Mauser shown here, together with its bayonet and scabbard.

SWEDISH MAUSER
SWEDISH MAUSER BAYONNET AND SHEATH
Sweden adopted the Mauser in 1893—although chambered for 6.65mm, a small round by the standards of military rifles of the era. The Swedes also insisted that while made in Germany, their Mausers be manufactured using Swedish steel.

The Automatic Pistol

The automatic pistol can be considered a stepchild of the machine gun. After Hiram Maxim (see p 115) figured out how to use a weapon's recoil to load, fire, eject, and reload a cartridge in the 1880s, weapons designers in several countries worked to scale down the system to the handgun level. (Strictly speaking, automatic pistols are really semiautomatic weapons, because they fire once with every trigger pull, and not continuously, like a machine gun—though fully automatic pistols have been developed.) Early automatics had some teething pains, particularly concerning cartridge size, but designers like John Browning (see sidebar) made the weapon viable.

BORCHARDT, BERGMANN, AND LUGER

The first successful automatic pistol was the brainchild of a German-born American inventor, Hugo Borchardt (1844–1924), who worked for several U.S. arms manufacturers, including Colt and Winchester. In 1893 Borchardt designed a pistol that used the Maxim recoil principle to send a toggle backward and upward to eject the spent cartridge and chamber a new one, fed from a magazine in the grip. (Reportedly, Borchardt's design was inspired by the movement of the human knee.) Borchardt found no takers for his pistol in America, so he moved to Germany, where the firm of Ludwig Loewe & Company brought the pioneering pistol on the market.

Also in Germany, around the same time, Austrian-born entrepreneur Theodor Bergmann (1850–1931) and the German designer Louis Schmeisser (1848–1917—father of Hugo Schmeisser) began developing a series of blowback-operated automatics, although these fed from a magazine in front of a trigger guard instead of in the grip—as did the "Broomhandle" Mauser developed around the same time.

Deutsch Waffen & Munitions Fabriken (DWM), the successor to Ludwig Loewe & Co., failed to sell the Borchardt pistol to the U.S. Army in the 1890s, but one of its employees, Georg Luger, improved on its design and eventually developed the first version of the famous pistol that would bear his name. The Swiss Army's adoption of the Luger in 1900 marked a major step forward in military acceptance of the automatic pistol. The German Army, however, considered the original Luger's 7.65mm round too weak. Luger then developed a new 9mm round (the parabellum, from the Latin "for war"). Germany adopted the 9mm version in 1908.

ENTER JOHN BROWNING

The main objection military customers had to the early automatics was the perceived lack of "stopping power" of their cartridges. (Automatic mechanisms couldn't function using the heavy revolver cartridges of the era.) In the early 1900s, the U.S. Army, however, found that even its .38 revolver was insufficient when used against determined Muslim insurgents in the Philippines (then an American colony). John Browning met the challenge with a pistol that, while automatic, fired an extremely powerful .45 round; the cartridge was called .45 ACP (Automatic Colt Pistol). Officially adopted by the U.S. Army in 1911, the Colt M1911 automatic went on to become one of the world's most successful and long-serving handguns.

BORCHARDT

Hugo Borchardt essentially designed his pistol, the first successful autoloader, around a new 7.65mm cartridge, which eventually became known as the 7.65 Mauser. The firing system was based around a locked breech; when fired, the barrel recoiled, unlocking the breechblock and activating a toggle that moved the barrel away from the breechblock, ejected the spent cartridge, and loaded a new one from the eight-round magazine in the grip. The awkward layout of the Borchardt, however, made it difficult to fire with one hand, so (like several other early automatics) it was supplied with a detachable stock.

BERGMANN

The blowback-operated
Bergmann automatics developed in
the mid-1890s (the Model 1894 is shown here)
were unusual in that they didn't incorporate an extraction
mechanism to eject spent cartridges; instead, the spent rounds
were blown out of the gun by gas pressure from the cartridge's firing.
The so-called "gas-extraction" mechanism made these pistols somewhat
prone to jamming. The Bergmann series were chambered for various calibers and had a revolver-
style grip, with rounds feeding from a magazine forward of the trigger guard. Later Bergmann
models included the "Mars" and "Simplex" automatics, which saw widespread military service
before and during World War I.

JOHN M. BROWNING

Browning was certainly the most
influential and versatile gunmaker of all
time. His work encompassed both civilian
and military weapons and includes
shotguns, machine guns, automatic rifles,
and automatic pistols. Indeed, many of his
designs are still in production today. John
Moses Browning was born in Ogden, Utah,
in 1855. Browning's
father, a gunsmith, was
among the Mormon pioneers
who had trekked westward to
Utah, and it was in his father's
shop that he built his first gun at
the age of thirteen. In 1883,
Browning went to work for Winchester,
where he designed several legendary
shotguns and rifles in the 1890s and early
1900s. His interest in automatic weapons
led to the development of a machine gun in
1895 and several automatic pistols, which
ultimately included the .45 M1911A1 Colt.
His .30 and .50 machine guns became
standard throughout the U.S. military, as
did the Browning Automatic Rifle (BAR). He
died in Belgium in 1926 while working on
the 9mm automatic pistol that would
eventually be produced as the Browning
High-Power (see p 128, image p 6).

LUGER

The Luger model adopted by the Swiss Army (like
the one shown here, with the Swiss Cross
stamped on the receiver) were in 7.65mm; the
German P08 model, adopted in 1908, fired the
9mm parabellum round which remains, almost a
century later, the most popular caliber for
automatic pistols and submachine guns. While
the Luger was undoubtedly an excellent weapon,
its legendary status—it was a coveted souvenir
among Allied troops in both world wars—
exaggerates its overall performance.

GLISENTI

First produced in 1910, the 9mm Glisenti (so-called from its manufacturer, Real Fabbrica d'Armi Glisenti) was the standard sidearm of the Italian Army in World War I. An overly complex firing system, combined with an unusual trigger mechanism, undercut its effectiveness.

ARTILLERY LUGER

Toward the end of World War I, the German Army introduced an interesting Luger variant—the so-called Artillery Model. The Artillery Luger had an 8in/20cm barrel instead of the standard model's 4in/10cm barrel, and was intended for use as a carbine with a wooden shoulder stock and a 32-round drum magazine (see p 127). As the name implies it was originally issued to gun crews as a defensive weapon, but it proved useful in the hands of trench-raiding infantry units.

COLT .45

"Tough, reliable, and packing a punch," in the words of firearms historian Craig Philip, "[Colt .45's] have endeared themselves to soldiers of all nations." At least 3 million of these pistols have been produced in the U.S., and an unknown number made under license (or simply copied) worldwide since its introduction in 1911. The original "government" model was slightly modified, based on combat experience in World War I, to become the M1911A1, which remained in U.S. military service until the mid-1980s. The weapon's main drawbacks were its heavy weight (2.5lb/1.1kg) and the fact that as a double-action weapon, it had to be carried with the slide pulled back in order to be ready to fire the first round quickly—something that could lead to accidental discharge in the hands of an inexperienced user.

BROOMHANDLE MAUSER

Mauser's first foray into automatic-pistol production came in 1896, with the introduction of a 7.63mm model which (along with its improved successor, the Model 1898) was popularly known as the "Broomhandle Mauser" from the distinctive design of its grip. Like the Borchardt and the Artillery Luger, the Broomhandle doubled as a carbine and came with a wooden stock that also served as a holster. One of the weapon's innovations was that the bolt remained open after the last of the ten rounds held in the box magazine was fired, facilitating reloading from a stripper clip. Broomhandles were a popular choice for private purchase by officers in several armies—among them a young British Army cavalryman named Winston Churchill, who used one in action at the Battle of Omdurman in the Sudan in 1898.

SCHWARZLOSE

Named for its designer, German Andreas Schwarzlose, the 9mm Schwarzlose Model 1908 automatic is virtually unique in that it uses a blow-forward operating system, with the slide moving forward rather than backward to load and eject each round. It was an effective system, but the novel experience of a pistol that recoiled away from, and not toward the firer surely took some getting used to. Schwarzlose also designed a well-regarded water-cooled machine gun, which was used by the Austro-Hungarian Army in World War II.

Personal Defense Weapons

Despite advances in public safety, such as the introduction of organized police forces, crime remained a major problem in Europe and the Americas in the nineteenth century. The rise of industrialization led to the massive growth of cities—and also the rise of an urban criminal underclass operating individually or in gangs—while bandits were still a threat in rural, isolated areas. As a result, some people armed themselves with small, easily concealable firearms for defense against robbers and the like—although the same type of weapon was frequently used by criminals themselves. With "gun control" more or less nonexistent at the time, such weapons were readily available for anyone—on either side of the law—who could afford them.

THE PERSONAL PISTOL

These weapons fall into several categories. Besides derringers (see pp 60–61), there were the so-called "pocket pistols," which, as the name implies, were meant to be carried clandestinely on the owner's person. Typically, these were short-barreled revolvers firing very small caliber rounds, often specially manufactured for a particular model of pistol. In order to be as compact as possible, many of these pistols had folding triggers and/or a completely enclosed hammer to reduce the danger of accidental discharge. The pocket-pistol concept continued in the twentieth century with the introduction of compact small-caliber automatics.

A subset of these weapons were "Lady's pistols" or "muff pistols," very small guns intended for use by women, which could be concealed in a handbag or in the fur muffs many women of the era wore as hand-warmers.

A more unusual category of weapon was the "palm" or "squeezer" pistols introduced in the late nineteenth century. These eschewed conventional pistol design in favor of a horizontally oriented weapon that could be concealed in the user's palm, with a "squeeze" firing mechanism replacing the standard trigger. The best-known models include the Belgian/French Le Merveilleux and Gauloise series and the American "Chicago Protector."

WALKING WEAPONS

While canes and walking sticks concealing dagger or sword blades were commonplace by the nineteenth century, the introduction of the percussion-cap firing system in the 1810s and 1820s made "cane guns" a practical weapon. In 1823, British gunsmith John Day patented a mechanism in which a downward pull on a hammer, concealed in the cane, dropped a trigger; thereafter, "Day's Patent" cane guns became the industry standard.

According to firearms historian Charles Edward Chapel, nineteenth-century cane guns were "made in large quantities for naturalists, gamekeepers, and poachers." Later in the century, cane guns firing the new fully enclosed metallic cartridge came into use, and while most cane guns of either firing system were single-shot, some cane revolvers were reportedly manufactured.

LADY'S PISTOL
Another example of the so-called "Lady's Pistol," this .22 revolver has a folding trigger and pearl-coated grips.

BELGIAN PALM PISTOL

This rare Belgian five-shot revolver has a grip designed to fit between the thumb and index finger like a wedge. In addition to the eccentric design, the pistol's folding trigger and double-action hammer are made of gold.

FRENCH PALM PISTOL

In the mid-1880s French gunmaker Jacques Rouchouse developed a palm pistol called Le Merveilleux. The design was triggerless; to fire, the user squeezed the frame, which activated the side-mounted hammer and discharged a specially made 6mm round. The same system was later used in pistols like the Gauloise series.

PROTECTOR PALM PISTOL

In 1882, French gunsmith Jacques Turbiaux patented a pistol designed to fit snugly in the palm; the cartridges (either ten 6mm rounds or seven 8mm) were contained in a horizontal radial cylinder. The design was licensed in the U.S. (firing a special short .32 round) by the Minneapolis Arms Company, and, later, by the Chicago Firearms Company, which marketed it as the "Chicago Protector."

BICYCLE PISTOL

The development of the modern "safety" bicycle in the 1880s touched off a craze for cycling in Europe and North America. Then as now, dogs did not always appreciate the presence of these vehicles on their territory. This .22 pistol, made in France around 1900, was intended for use by bicyclists to frighten dogs; it can fire both blanks and live rounds.

BABY REVOLVER

Starting in the late 1800s, Philadelphia gunmaker Henry Kolb produced a series of ultra-compact, hammerless "Baby" revolvers. This .22 folding-trigger model is nickel-plated with pearl grips.

COACHING CARBINE

This nineteenth-century British percussion "coaching carbine"—so called because it would have been carried by a stagecoach driver or guard to ward off highwaymen—is double-barreled and incorporates a short spring bayonet.

PATTI PINFIRE REVOLVER
This single-shot, .30 pin-fire pistol with a folding trigger was owned by Adelina Patti (1843–1919). Born in Spain to Italian parents, Patti was one of the great operatic sopranos of her era.

MUFF PISTOLS
As the name implies, these Belgian-made, ivory-handled .36 single-shot percussion "muff pistols" were intended to be carried in a lady's hand-warming muff.

WEAPONS OF DECEPTION

LANE CANE GUN

One of the rarest examples of this type of
weapon is the nineteeth-century percussion-
cap British Lane Cane Gun. The upper part of
the cane, which contained the gun, was
detached from the lower part and could be
fired from the shoulder.

UMBRELLA GUN

A nineteenth-century percussion-cap gun disguised as an umbrella. A modern version of the umbrella gun—in this case, firing a projectile coated with the toxic agent Ricin—was used to assassinate a Bulgarian dissident in London in 1978 (see also 134–35).

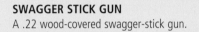

SWAGGER STICK GUN

A .22 wood-covered swagger-stick gun.

HIKING-STICK GUN

This British gentleman's nineteenth-century hiking stick does double duty with its detachable percussion-cap single shot.

WALKING-STICK GUN

A nineteenth-century English walking-stick gun. The weapon contains a single-shot percussion-cap firing mechanism, a system devised by British gunsmith John Day.

Combination Weapons

Weapons that combine a firearm with a blade or a club—or all three—have a pedigree that goes back to the sixteenth century. Until the advent of practical repeating firearms toward the middle of the nineteenth century, guns (unless they were multiple-barreled) could only fire one shot before reloading, therefore, giving the user an additional means of dispatching an opponent (or defending himself against said opponent) was a concern of weapons-makers. The introduction of repeating arms didn't completely end this trend; in the late nineteenth century, there was a vogue for revolver/dagger or knife combinations, and the famous (or infamous) French "Apache" managed to combine a revolver, a knife blade, and a set of brass knuckles in a single weapon. Combination weapons in our own time include "drillings" (a double-barreled shotgun with a rifle barrel—usually of European manufacture); combination guns (one shotgun barrel, one rifle barrel), and the survival guns (incorporating a small-caliber rifle and a shotgun) developed by the air forces of several nations as hunting weapons for downed aircrew stranded in remote areas awaiting rescue.

DIRK PISTOL
The Belgian-French gunmakers Dumonthier & Sons produced several knife-pistol combinations, like the one shown here, which has a 13.5in/34cm blade mounted above double barrels. Dumonthier also manufactured a number of cane guns (see pp 94–95).

TRUNCHEON GUN
This nineteenth-century British weapon combines a truncheon (club) with a decorated head with a percussion-cap pistol. It uses the firing system devised by British gunsmith John Day for his celebrated cane guns (see pp 94–95).

DAGGER PISTOL
While disguised as a dagger, this Japanese weapon is actually a single-shot percussion-cap pistol.

BATTLE-AX-GUN
Made in India around 1830, this weapon combines a battle-ax and a percussion-cap gun.

KNIFE PISTOL
The London firm of Unwin & Rodgers, a pioneer in knife-pistol combinations, made this pocket-knife pistol in the early 1870s. It incorporates a .36, muzzle-loading, single-shot pistol and two folding blades.

TURKISH GUN-SHIELD
Engraved across its entire surface and partly inlayed with gold and silver, this shield—16in/41cm in diameter—incorporates a percussion-cap gun in a wooden mount on the reverse side, with a 5in/13cm protruding barrel. Pulling a string discharged the gun.

INDIAN SHIELD WITH PISTOLS
The innocuous-looking "aged" shield hides four barrels behind its bosses, which swivel away to shoot a deadly deluge of bullets. It dates from the nineteenth century and is composed of hand-hammered steel.

ETHIOPIAN SHIELD
Some Persian shields have spikes in their center to use in combat. The one barrel protruding from the middle of this shield looks like a spike at a distance. Only at close (shooting) range is it recognizable as a gun barrel.

KNIFE REVOLVER

Another European combination weapon features a six-shot, double-action revolver with folding, curved-blade knife.

APACHE

One of the rarest and yet most famous combination weapons of the nineteenth century was the "Apache," so-called because it was supposedly used by Parisian gangsters who took the name of the warlike Native American nation. (Firearms historian Charles Edward Chapel considered its name "a gross libel on American Apache Indians.") The "Apache" combined a revolver (usually 7mm pinfire, apparently), a folding blade of about 3.5in/9cm, and a "brass knuckle" grip (see p 96). Given the shortness of the blade and the fact that the pistol component didn't even have a barrel, it's effectiveness as either a firearm or a knife is pretty doubtful.

INDIAN COMBO

Talk about multitasking: This nineteenth-century weapon—custom-made for an Indian prince—incorporates a sword; a shield; a single-shot, percussion-cap pistol; and a 12in/30.5cm needle dagger. It was made of steel with gold inlay and brass embellishments.

INDIAN MACE/PISTOL
In the nineteenth century, an Indian gunsmith fitted this mace—which may have been made more than two centuries earlier—with a percussion-cap gun.

NINETEENTH-CENTURY COMBO
Another unusual nineteenth-century multi-use weapon—this one of European origin—includes a knife blade, single-shot pistol, and a shaft reinforced with metal for use as a club.

COMBO PISTOL DAGGER
This Belgian pistol (in formidable .80) includes not one but two knife blades—a 6.5in/16.5cm straight blade that slides forward from the frame, and an 8in/20cm curved blade concealed in the buttstock. In addition, the trigger guard is lengthened and reinforced to parry the sword or knife-thrust of an attacker.

CUTLASS PISTOL

Dumonthier also made this single-shot, .31 percussion-cap pistol with a cutlass blade; the pistol barrel and blade are forged from the same piece of metal.

MARBLE GAME-GETTER

Introduced in 1908 by the Marble Safety Axe Company (later Marble's Arms & Manufacturing) of Michigan, the "Game Getter" was a folding-stock, over-and-under double-barreled weapon, with the upper barrel chambered for .22 cartridges and the lower barrel chambered for .44 (later .410) shotgun shells. The idea was to give hunters a single compact weapon suitable for dealing with both birds and four-legged game.

Alarm, Trap, and Special-Purpose Guns

Not all guns are made to kill. From the introduction of gunpowder, various firearms have been used for purposes like signaling, timekeeping, and sounding alarms. The number of these special-purpose guns grew after the introduction of the percussion cap in the first half of the nineteenth century. These pages present some interesting examples from the era.

ALARM AND TRAP GUNS

The alarm gun was developed to give homeowners a means of warding off burglars. Usually they were attached to windows or doors; when an intruder tried to open these, a trip wire would activate a percussion cap and fire a powder charge, or in later versions, fire a blank cartridge, alerting the homeowner and, presumably, sending the intruder fleeing. One variation consisted of a small-caliber, blank-firing pistol attached via a screw to a door or window frame, which would discharge when the door or window was opened.

Trap guns—also known as spring guns—were most commonly deployed in rural areas against poachers. Like many alarm guns, they were activated by trip wires, but unlike alarm guns, some of them were intended to fire bullets or shot instead of powder charges or blanks.

LINE-THROWING AND SIGNAL GUNS

At sea it was often necessary for one ship to get a line onto the deck of another, whether to take a damaged vessel in tow or to send across messages or supplies. This led to the development of line-throwing guns, like the pistol version shown on page 99. Coast Guards and lifeboatmen also used line-throwing cannon—like the famous U.S. Lyle Gun, used from the late nineteenth century until the 1950s—to fire lines onto wrecked ships in order to bring passengers and crew safely ashore.

Before the introduction of radio, it was customary for both merchant vessels and warships to announce their arrival in port by firing signal guns, and it was also often necessary for ships to signal to one another with guns when fog and other weather conditions made visual signaling with flags impossible. Because firing a ship's "big guns" for such purposes was impractical, many ships carried small signal cannons like the one shown on page 99.

WALLIS ALARM GUN
This nineteenth-century alarm gun was manufactured by the Hull, England, gunsmithing firm of John Wallis. The hammer was cocked by a double-ended trip bar; when this bar was tripped by an intruder, the device set off a percussion cap.

NAYLOR TRAP GUN

Another English gunsmith, Isaac Naylor, patented this "Alarm Gun or Reporter and Detector" in 1836. It comprised a steel block with vertical chambers that were loaded with gunpowder; a percussion-cap firing mechanism was activated by the leaf-spring striker at the bottom of the device when triggered by a trip wire. The horizontal hole bored through the block allowed the device to be firmly anchored to the ground with stakes. Various models of the gun have between one and six barrels.

LINE-THROWING PISTOL

A Royal Navy percussion cap line-throwing pistol from around 1860. A small line was attached to the brass rod in the barrel and fired from one ship to another using a blank cartridge; once the small line was secured, it would be used to pull across a thicker rope or cable.

NINETEENTH-CENTURY NAVAL CANNON

This nineteenth-century naval signal cannon was used for both signaling and saluting. Similar small cannon were also used for timekeeping—by firing to mark noon, for example—on land. The British Royal Navy started the custom of firing cannon salutes, and being the most formidable presence at sea, compelled ships of other nations to fire salutes first, after which the English ship would respond in kind.

GREENER'S HUMANE CATTLE KILLER

The venerable English gunmaker W W Greener—set up in 1855, later absorbing his late father's business (founded in 1829)—made this interesting device. Marketed as "Greener's Humane Cattle Killer," it was designed to do just that—quickly kill cattle or put down a horse injured beyond hope of recovery. The user unscrewed the cap at the top, inserted a .310 cartridge, replaced the cap, and placed the wide end against the horse's forehead with the notch pointing upward, keeping the barrel in line with the spinal column, so that the bullet will enter the medulla, killing the horse instantly. These were issued to veterinarians accompanying British Army cavalry units in World War I. W W Greener continues to make high-quality arms.

PART III

World War I and Its Aftermath

"But that he has not taken with him his sword red with blood as he intended,—that he has left us alive,—that we wrested the weapon from his hands,—that he has left the citizens safe and the city standing, what great and overwhelming grief must you think that this is to him!"

—Cicero, "The Second Oration Against Catiline," 63 BCE

World War I (1914–18) saw the convergence of the weapons technologies that had developed over the previous century or so—with horrific results for soldiers in all the armies involved. The bolt-action rifle was by now the standard infantryman's weapon, but this war would be dominated not by the rifle but by heavy, crew-served machine guns and rapid-firing artillery delivering heavy explosive and shrapnel shells. The early battlefields of the Western Front proved so deadly that both sides dug in, until a continuous line of trenches snaked across Belgium and France.

World War I also saw the introduction of new weapons like tanks, aircraft, flamethrowers, and—perhaps most terrifying—poison gas. The success of the machine gun, and the need for a weapon that would be more effective in trench fighting than conventional rifles, led armies to experiment with automatic weapons that could be carried into combat by individuals, including automatic rifles and submachine guns, although these innovations arrived too late to make much of a difference.

Pistols of World War I

In World War I, pistols were carried chiefly by officers and NCOs. They remained a standard cavalry weapon, as they'd been for centuries, but mounted troops played little role in World War I. Still, pistols were prized by frontline infantrymen for use in close combat; they also were carried by tank crews, aircrew, and support troops as a defensive weapon in conditions that made the use of a rifle impractical.

THE REVOLVER

By the time World War I began in 1914 the automatic pistol (see pp 86–89) was finally winning acceptance among the world's armed forces. Switzerland and Germany, for example, had adopted the 9mm Luger, while the U.S. (which would enter the war in 1917) adopted the Colt .45 automatic in 1911. Many military officers, however, believed (with some justification) that automatics, which are far more complicated mechanically than revolvers, weren't reliable or rugged enough to withstand the rigors of muddy, dusty, and damp combat conditions. Throughout the war, the British Army remained strongly devoted to the revolvers made by the Birmingham firm of Webley & Scott, which first entered service in the 1880s; the French used the Lebel revolver, and the Russians, the Nagant—although pistols of any kind were in short supply in the under-equipped Russian Army. Also, most automatics of the era were chambered for the 7.65mm or 9mm cartridge, which supposedly had less "stopping power" than heavier .38 or .45/.455 revolver rounds—.45/.455 being equivalent of 11mm.

BERGMANN-BAYARD M1910

Designed by Danish gunmaker Theodore Bergmann (see p 86) and his associates, the Bergmann-Bayard M1910 was a 9mm automatic that could take either a six- or ten-round magazine. Besides being the official Danish sidearm, it was adopted by the armies of Belgium, Greece, and Spain. They were also widely used by the Danish resistance movement during the German occupation of that country in World War II.

GERMAN REVOLVER

Despite the adoption of the Luger, many German cavalrymen of World War I carried six-shot, .44 revolvers like the one shown here. The ring on the butt accommodated a lanyard that secured the pistol to the trooper's clothing or gear.

GLISENTI M1910 AUTO
Manufactured by the firm of Real Fabbrica d'Armi Glisenti, the Model 1910 automatic was a mainstay of Italian forces in World War I. The M1910, however, had an overly complicated firing system that required the use of a weaker version of the 9mm round, which limited its range and stopping power.

STEYR
The Steyr 9mm automatic was the standard pistol of the Austro-Hungarian armies in World War I and many later found their way into the Wehrmacht in World War II. Like the "snail drum" Luger shown (see p 127), this particular pistol was captured during the Allied campaign against German and Italian forces in North Africa.

"They shall not pass."

—General Pétain, Battle of Verdun, 1916

Infantry Rifles of World War I

From the turn of the twentieth century, military rifle technology advanced at a slower pace than that of other weapons. The World War I infantryman in most armies went into battle carrying a rifle with a design pedigree dating back to the mid-nineteenth century.

IF AIN'T BROKE ...
There were valid reasons for this relative conservatism. Bolt-action rifles were sturdy, and mechanically simple, and accurate over long distances—typically up to 500–600yd/1650–1980 meters. The main trend in rifle development before World War I was simply to make infantry rifles shorter and lighter, blurring the nineteenth-century distinction between rifle and carbine: Examples include the U.S. Springfield M1903, the British SMLE (Short Magazine Lee-Enfield) and the German KAR-98.

Although a well-trained soldier could get off about 15 shots per minute with World War I–era bolt-action rifles, weapons designers were already working on semiautomatic rifles to increase the volume of infantry firepower. (Operating by means of recoil or from the energy of the gas created as a fired cartridge left the barrel, semiautomatic rifles—also known as autoloading rifles—fire once for every pull of the trigger.)

SEMIAUTOMATICS ARRIVE
From the mid-1890s onward, the military establishments of Denmark, Mexico, Germany, Russia, and Italy experimented with semiautomatic rifles, but none saw widespread use. Experimentation continued, but adoption of the semiautomatic rifle was slowed by the same concerns over replacement of revolvers with automatic pistols (see p 86)—the relative complexity of semiautomatic rifles compared to bolt-action rifles, and the fact that most semiautomatics fired a lighter, shorter cartridge. In addition, officers worried that troops armed with rapid-fire rifles would expend their ammunition too quickly.

KAR-98
The 7.92mm KAR-98 (for karabiner, model 1998) was the standard German infantry rifle in both world wars. It used the classic forward-locking Mauser bolt action, weighed 8.5lb/3.9kg, and had an integral 5-round box magazine.

EDDYSTONE ENFIELD
The U.S. entered World War I in April 1917 with an arms industry woefully unprepared to equip a large army. Because of difficulties in expanding production of the standard U.S. Army rifle, the M1903 Springfield, the army also adopted a rifle based on the British Enfield, because the latter weapon was already in production in the U.S. under contract. The result was the U.S. Rifle Model 1917—basically, an Enfield with an action and magazine modified for the U.S .30 cartridges.

"INDIAN PATTERN" BAYONET
Many early SMLEs were issued with an impractically long and cumbersome sword-style bayonet. Historian Pierre Berton notes that during World War I, Canadian troops considered this particular model of bayonet useless for anything except toasting bread over campfires.

MKII BAYONET

This spike-type bayonet was made for use with one of the SMLE's successors, the SMLE Mark IV, during World War II. It was manufactured by the U.S. firm of Stevens-Savage under contract with the British government.

ENFIELD

With a design incorporating lessons learned in the Boer War (1899–1902), the first version of the .303 SMLE (Short Magazine Lee-Enfield), the Mark III, entered service with the British Army in 1907. The SMLE's action gave it a high rate of fire relative to other rifles of the time, and it had a 10-round magazine. When German troops came under British fire early in World War I, the British put up such a sustained, rapid fire that the Germans believed they were under attack by machine guns.

US GAS MASK

Poison gas was one of World War I's special horrors. Both the French and the German armies used irritant gases (i.e., tear gas) early in the war, but gas warfare entered a more deadly phase during the Battle of Ypres in April 1915, when the Germans wafted chlorine gas toward British trenches. Soon both sides used gases, mainly delivered by artillery shells. Some gases (like mustard gas) disabled victims; others (like phosgene) were often immediately fatal. Early countermeasures were crude—such as holding urine-soaked cotton wadding over the nose and mouth—but as the war went on, increasingly effective gas masks, or "respirators," were developed. The one shown here was issued to U.S. troops.

MORTARS

Sometimes called "the infantryman's artillery," compact, mobile mortars developed during World War I to give supporting fire to riflemen in both offense and defensive operations, and they remain in service in many armies today. Typically produced in 60mm, 80mm, and 120mm versions, the mortar is just a tube that delivers plunging fire by launching a grenade-like projectile with a propelling charge in its base. Shown here are (right) The French Model 1937 mortar used in World War II, and a Finnish mortar (above).

LEBEL BAYONET

This bayonet was produced in 1916 for use with the 8mm French Lebel Model 1886 bolt-action rifle. The metal grip was produced in both nickel and brass, as supplies of the metals dictated.

VETTERLI-VITALI

During World War I, the Italian Army modified numbers of its elderly Model 71 carbines—originally single-shot, 10.4mm weapons—into more feasible 6.5mm rifles fed by the same 6-round magazine used by the Mannlicher-Carcano M1891.

JAPANESE PARATROOP RIFLE

Because the standard 7.7mm Arisaka rifle was too long for use in airborne operations, the Japanese military developed a special version for paratroops that could be broken down into two pieces for the jump and then reassembled on landing. Relatively few saw service.

MOSIN-NAGANT M91/30/59

Drawing on design elements provided by the Russian Colonel Sergei Mosin and Belgian Leon Nagant, the 7.62mm, bolt-action Mosin-Nagant would, in various models and upgrades, remain the standard Russian (and later Soviet) infantry rifle from the early 1890s until around 1950.

RUSSIAN CARBINE M1944

The Mosin-Nagant Carbine M944, introduced toward the end of World War II, was the final iteration of the Mosin-Nagant series. Its most distinctive feature was an integral bayonet that folded into the stock.

MANNLICHER-CARCANO

Although they bear the name of the Austro-German gun designer Ferdinand Ritter von Mannlicher, the Mannlicher-Carcano series of 6.5mm carbines and rifles—the mainstay of the Italian armed forces from 1891 through World War II—were actually based on a Mauser design. (The "Carcano" designation is for Salvatore Carcano, a designer at the Italian government arsenal at Turin). The Model 1941 rifle is shown here. The Mannlicher-Carcano gained postwar notoriety in 1963, when Lee Harvey Oswald used a ML carbine he'd purchased through the mail to assassinate U.S. president John F. Kennedy.

Machine Guns of World War I

The concept of an automatic weapon—one that would fire continuously for as long as the operator pulled back the trigger—goes back to at least 1718, when Englishmen James Puckle proposed a multi-cylinder "defence gun." Several manually operated rapid-fire guns were introduced in the mid-nineteenth century. Some, like the U.S. Gatling gun (see p 73) were relatively successful. Others, like the French Mitrailleuse, were not. The first modern machine gun, the Maxim gun, appeared in 1885 (see sidebar). First used in large numbers in the Russo-Japanese War (1904–05), the machine gun changed warfare forever during World War I, and it remains a principal weapon of the world's arsenals in the twenty-first century.

THE BIRTH OF THE MACHINE GUN

Although it had competition from weapons like the British Gardner gun and the Swedish Nordenfeldt gun, the Maxim design was adopted by a number of nations from the 1880s through the early 1900s. Appearing at the high point of European imperialism, the Maxim and other rapid-fire guns proved useful in slaughtering indigenous peoples in colonial conflicts, prompting British writer Hilaire Belloc to rhyme sardonically: "Whatever happens, we have got/The Maxim gun, and they have not."

Then came World War I. Though the British Army had been among the first to adopt the machine gun, it went into action underequipped with the weapon and underestimating its effects, while the French were convinced that "the spirit of the attack" would overcome automatic fire. The German Army did not labor under these misapprehensions, however, and the Allies suffered accordingly—but would rapidly catch up in the firepower sweepstakes.

As many historians have noted, most brilliantly John Ellis in his *The Social History of the Machine Gun*, the devastation wrought by the machine gun in World War I had a psychological as well as a physical aspect. The machine gun reduced killing to an industrial process. It represented the nexus of the Industrial Revolution and the age of mass warfare. Future British Prime Minister Winston Churchill—who spent ninety days as an infantry officer in the trenches of the Western Front—was certainly thinking of the machine gun when he wrote, in a postwar memoir, "War, which used to be cruel and magnificent, has now become cruel and squalid . . ."

MARLIN MACHINE GUN

When the U.S. entered World War I in April 1917, the U.S. Army contracted Marlin Arms to produce a version of the .30 Colt-Browning Model 1895 machine gun, which was already in use by the Navy. Designed by the great John Browning (see p 87), the gun had a big disadvantage in infantry combat: The gas system used a piston that moved back and forth below the barrel, so it could be fired only from a fairly high tripod mount—thus exposing the crew to enemy fire. Because of the piston's tendency to hit the ground below, troops nicknamed it the "potato-digger."

LEWIS LIGHT MACHINE GUN

The British Army went into World War I using a couple of American machine-gun designs, including the Lewis Light Machine Gun. Developed by U.S. Army officer Noah Lewis in 1911, the .303, gas-operated weapon was fed by a tubular 50-round top-mounted magazine, and it had a distinctive "shroud" to cool the barrel. It was widely used to arm Allied aircraft, and a .30 version was developed for U.S. forces.

SIR HIRAM MAXIM

Born in Maine in 1840, Hiram Maxim became a prolific inventor at an early age, patenting—among other items—the proverbial "better mousetrap." While attending an industrial exhibition in Paris in 1881, a friend told him that if he really wanted to make a fortune, he should "invent something that will enable these Europeans to cut each other's throats with greater facility." Maxim took these words to heart, and a few years later he unveiled the gun that would bear his name. Fed by a continuous belt of ammunition (initially .45, later .303), the Maxim gun was recoil-operated; the operator cocked and fired the weapon, and the recoil ejected the spent cartridge and chambered a new round. Because the rapid rate of fire—up to 600 rounds per minute—could melt the barrel, he surrounded it with a jacket filled with water. (Later "air-cooled" machine guns would use a perforated metal jacket.) The Maxim design was soon adopted by several nations, including Britain, and reportedly, turn-of-the-twentieth century Maxims were being used by the Chinese Army in the Korean War more than a half-century later. Maxim took British citizenship and, in 1901, was knighted for his services.

FRENCH CHAUCHET

One of World War I's worst weapons, France's Chauchat automatic rifle was poorly made from sub-standard components, and it was fed by 8mm Lebel rifle cartridges from a crescent-shaped magazine, an inaccurate and unreliable system for an automatic weapon. When U.S. troops arrived on the Western Front, they were equipped with large numbers of this weapon re-chambered for the American .30 round. In addition to its inherent faults, most of these guns were mechanically clapped-out from years of service. American soldiers and marines—who called the weapon the "Cho-Cho"—considered it worse than useless, and they usually were left behind before going into action.

COLT VICKERS

Shortly before World War I, the British Army adopted the Vickers gun as its standard heavy machine gun. A .303 water-cooled gun based on the basic Maxim design, the weapon's biggest drawback was its weight—83lb/37.7kg with its tripod. It typically required a crew of six to carry and operate.

GERMAN SPANDAU MAXIM

Officially the Maxim LMG 08/15, the "Spandau" got its nickname from one of Imperial Germany's arsenals. The 7.92mm, water-cooled, belt-fed weapon was the standard armament for German aircraft from 1915 on, after the development of the "interrupter gear," which synchronized the weapon's firing rate with the revolution of the aircraft's propeller, allowing the gun to shoot safely through the plane's propeller arc.

Trench Warfare

In 1897, a Polish-Jewish financier named Ivan Bloch (c. 1832–1902) published a book titled *The War of the Future*. Bloch contended that given the combination of mass conscript armies and weapons like machine guns and quick-firing artillery firing explosive shells, any European conflict would degenerate into a war of attrition fought by soldiers burrowing into the earth for protection. His theory was ignored or scoffed at. Not much more than a decade after his death, he would be proved a prophet. Even after the horrors of World War II and the nuclear knife-edge of the Cold War, the misery and deadliness of the trench warfare of World War I haunts the Western world into the twenty-first century.

THE WESTERN FRONT

Trench warfare was not new in 1914. During the American Civil War (1861–65), the effectiveness of the rifled musket (see p 111) was such that both sides learned the value of "digging in." Indeed, photographs of the Union Army's lines around Petersburg, Virginia—the gateway to the Confederate capital at Richmond—in 1864–65 are eerily similar to photographs of the Western Front in France and Belgium fifty years later.

Observers from European armies failed to learn any lessons from that conflict. When World War I broke out in Europe in August 1914, the French Army still held to the doctrine of *"L'Attaque! Toujours l'attaque!"* ("The attack—always the attack!"), believing that a spirited offense over open ground would always overwhelm the enemy. In the opening months of the conflict, the French managed to hold the Germans attackers on the Marne River and save Paris from capture, but their tactics cost hundreds of thousands of lives.

Thereafter the French and their British allies established a line of trenches that stretched nearly 500 miles from the English Channel to the Swiss border, separated from the German trenches by a "no-man's-land" that in places was no more than a few hundred feet or even less.

LIFE AND DEATH IN THE TRENCHES

These trenches ranged from mere scratched-out ditches to (especially on the largely defensive German side) elaborate positions with bunkers well below ground to give protection from shellfire. In general, though, trench lines consisted of forward trenches directly facing the enemy, backed by a couple of lines of support trenches, connected to each other and to the rear by communication trenches. Beds of barbed wire protected the forward trenches, which also had extensions known as saps for placement of machine guns, snipers, and observation posts to keep tabs on the enemy.

For soldiers in all armies, life in the trenches was miserable, so much so that whenever possible units were rotated to rear areas after a few days or weeks on the front line. They had to endure cold, wet, lice, and rats—the last often bloated from feeding on corpses. Uninterrupted sleep was impossible thanks to snipers and artillery barrages. Even in the quiet periods between major offensives, there was a steady stream of casualties from conditions like "trench foot" (caused by prolonged immersion of the feet in the water that inevitably collected in the bottom of trenches) and among men sent into "no-man's-land" each night to install or repair barbed wire, or on combat patrols against enemy positions to seize prisoners for questioning. The British referred to these attritional casualties as "normal wastage." And besides these miseries, there was the ever-present threat of gas (see p 71), and the psychological injuries—dubbed "shell shock"—as men broke down from hardship, the strain of combat, and particularly, the shattering effects of artillery bombardment.

WEAPONS OF TRENCH WARFARE

For hundreds of years, infantry had generally been the decisive factor on European battlefields, but in World War I artillery achieved preeminence. At the Third Battle of Ypres in 1917, for example, British artillery fired a staggering 4.7 million shells over three weeks. The intent, in this as in many other battles, was to "soften" the enemy in preparation for infantry assault across no-man's-land. However, these bombardments rarely achieved their purpose. Dug deep into the ground, the Germans were usual able to emerge with their machine guns intact and ready to scour the advancing Allied infantry. On the first day of the First Battle of the Somme—July 1, 1916—for example, British forces suffered 58,000 casualties, one-third of them deaths. By the time the offensive halted four months later, the British had lost 420,000 men in all—for a gain of 7.5km/12mi.

In an effort to break the deadlock on the Western Front, the British developed a new weapon—the tank, a tracked, armored "land battleship." While tanks had some success, especially at the Battle of Cambrai (November 20–December 7, 1917), they didn't prove a decisive factor in the war. For their part, the Germans sought to break the deadlock by developing tactics based around small groups of *strosstruppen* (literally, "storm troops") armed with new weapons like flamethrowers and submachine guns (see pp 134–35).

Despite these innovations, some weapons of trench warfare were throwbacks to the past. Personal armor reappeared in the form of steel helmets; raiding parties carried improvised pole arms, clubs, and edged weapons; and the hand grenade—whose use had declined after the eighteenth century—once again became an important part of the infantryman's personal arsenal.

In the end, attrition prevailed. In the spring of 1918, the Germans launched a series of offensives aimed at knocking out the British and French before large numbers of American troops (the U.S. had entered the war a year earlier) arrived in France. They narrowly failed. The guns finally fell silent at 11:00 a.m. on November 11, 1918—by which time the trenches of the Western Front had become graves for millions of young men.

THE BATTLE OF BROODSEINDE

Guns of the American Roaring Twenties

In January 1920, Prohibition—a federal ban on the "manufacture, sale, or transportation" of alcohol—went into effect in the United States. Intended to stop the crime and social ills associated with drinking, this "noble experiment" backfired badly. People still wanted to drink, "bootleggers" were willing to make or smuggle alcohol, and organized crime, sniffing rich profits, stepped in to control the trade in illicit hooch. Throughout the 1920s and beyond, gangsters fought each other and the authorities using a variety of powerful weapons, forcing law-enforcement agencies to catch up in the firepower stakes.

THE TOMMY GUN

The most iconic weapon of the 1920s is surely the Thompson Submachine Gun. Much to the embarrassment of its inventor, John T. Thompson (see sidebar), who had developed it for military use, the weapon was eagerly taken up by gangsters in Chicago and other cities and put to deadly use in their battles with rival gangs and with the authorities. (Given the lax gun-control laws of the era, obtaining weapons—even automatic weapons—was not difficult for criminals.)

The Thompson soon earned a variety of nicknames, including the "Tommy Gun," the "Chicago typewriter," and the "chopper." Perhaps the Thompson's most notorious application came in the "St. Valentine's Day Massacre" of 1929, when members of Al Capone's gang murdered seven associates of a rival concern in a Chicago garage. The power of the Thompson's .45 ACP rounds at close range was such that several of the victim's bodies were reportedly cut nearly in half.

PISTOLS IN POCKETS, BANDITS ON WHEELS

The success of the Thompson in outlaw hands led many law-enforcement agencies, including the FBI, to finally purchase the weapon; the Thompson would be part of the "G-Men's" arsenal for decades. The FBI also made use of the BAR (see p 133). Most local police forces, however, remained armed solely with revolvers and shotguns—giving the lawmen a distinctive disadvantage when gangsters came to town.

Another weapons development of the 1920s was the widespread adoption of "pocket pistols" by criminals. These were small automatic pistols, usually in .22 or .25 caliber, which, as the name implies, could be easily concealed in a coat pocket, ankle holster, or tucked behind the belt in the small of the back. They were handy weapons in case a bootlegging deal went bad, or in last-ditch struggles to escape the police.

Prohibition ended in 1933, but the Great Depression saw the rise of a new breed of outlaw: The "motorized bandits" who roamed the roads of the Midwest and Southwest commiting crime. Such felons included the Barker Gang, John Dillinger, "Pretty Boy" Floyd, and Bonnie Parker and Clyde Barrow. These outlaws also made use of the Thompson, sawed-off shotguns, and even the BAR, the latter sometimes in cut-down form.

MITRAILLEUSE
This highly unusual gun, dubbed a "window revolver" was made in France as a defensive weapon; it was fitted to a window or barricade, and the firer, under cover, pulled a string attached to the lever to fire and advance each of the 24 cylinders. By some accounts, Al Capone's gang mounted the gun on the bows of the motorboats used to bring in illegal booze from Canada in case they encountered U.S. Customs patrols or other authorities. This would have been impractical under these circumstances, as the weapon could only be aimed by steering the boat directly at the target.

COLT POLICE POSITIVE
By the 1920s many U.S. policemen and private armed guards carried .32 or .38 Colt "Police Positive" revolvers. The name came from a new safety feature, introduced in 1905, which separated the hammer from the firing pin, thus reducing the chances of accidental discharge. This particular .38 was manufactured for use by security guards of Wells Fargo & Co.

LILIPUT PISTOL

The Liliput series of automatic pistols made by Waffenfabrik August Menz in Germany was aptly named—this one measures 3.5 in./8.9cm long; to keep the weapon as small as possible, Menz chambered it for the rare 4.25mm round. (Other, slightly larger Liliput models used a 6.35mm round.) The 1927 4.25mm is shown here.

J. T. THOMPSON

Born in Kentucky in 1860, John Taliaferro Thompson graduated from West Point and served as an artillery officer before joining the U.S. Army's Ordnance Department. During his long tenure, Thompson played a key role in the development of the Springfield M1903 rifle and the Colt M1911 pistol. During World War I, Thompson became convinced that the Allies needed a handheld automatic weapon—which he dubbed a "trench broom"—to break the stalemate on the Western Front, and he set up a firm, the Auto-Ordnance Company, to manufacture such a gun. The result was the Thompson Submachine Gun. Unfortunately, the gun went into production too late to see service, leaving Auto-Ordnance with a large inventory. Thompson tried to sell the weapon to police forces, with only modest success. As a result, he lost control of Auto-Ordnance. Thompson died in 1940, just as the Thompson came into its own as an Allied weapon in a new world war.

GAS BILLY CLUB

A real rarity: Federal Laboratories Inc. of Pittsburgh, Pennsylvania, produced this combination billy club/tear-gas launcher for police use in the mid-1920s.

PARKER BROTHERS SHOTGUN

In the prosperous 1920s, many Americans adopted skeet shooting and fowl hunting as a hobby. Parker Brothers of Meriden, Connecticut, made this 20-gauge shotgun in 1928. Made especially for women shooters, it is lightweight (6lb/2.7kg) and has a lighter trigger pull than the standard model.

THOMPSON

The Thompson submachine used a delayed-blowback operation developed by U.S. Navy officer John Blish. It fired the same .45 ACP cartridge as the Colt M1911 pistol and fed either from a 50-round drum magazine or a 20 (later 30)-round box magazine. Hollywood forever linked the "Tommy Gun" with U.S. gang wars of the 1920s in the public mind, but the weapon also first saw military service during the decade. The Irish Republican Army (IRA) in the Irish Civil War of the early 1920s also used the Thompson; in 1928, the U.S. Navy adopted the gun as the M1928A1 (the model shown here), and marines used it to fight a leftist insurgency in Nicaragua. It was later adopted by the U.S. Army and remained the standard U.S. submachine well into World War II, in the M1A1 model, which simplified some aspects of the action and eliminated the forward grip and the capacity to take the drum magazine. An excellent weapon, the Thompson's chief drawbacks were its weight (over 10lb/4.5kg) and its manufacturing cost.

"Wars may be fought with weapons, but they are won by men. It is the spirit of men who follow and of the man who leads that gains the victory."

—General George S. Patton

To a great extent, World War II (1939–45) was fought with weapons that had their antecedents in World War I. Automatic pistols, already in widespread use during the earlier conflict, replaced the revolver as the standard military sidearm. Submachine guns—from the U.S. Thompson to the German MP40 "Schmeisser" to the cheap and simple Ppsh 41 used by the Soviet Red Army—joined the infantry's arsenal. The years preceding the war also saw various nations experimenting with semi-automatic, or self-loading, rifles to replace bolt-action models, but only the U.S. Army made such a weapon its standard rifle during the war itself, in the form of the M1 Garand.

During the war, Germany developed the MP44 Sturmgewher ("assault rifle"), an innovative weapon that combined the rapid-fire capabilities of the submachine gun with the range and "stopping power" of the rifle. The MP44 is the direct ancestor of the assault rifles that became the dominant infantry weapon of the postwar world, the outstanding examples being the AK47 (first produced in the Soviet Union, but manufactured worldwide in huge numbers and in several variations) and the U.S. M16.

Axis Pistols

With little room for improvement in revolver design, the interwar years saw automatics become the standard sidearm in most armies. The Soviet Union adopted the Tokarev, which the great weapons writer Ian Hogg described as a "[Colt] M1911 with a distinctive Russian accent." In Japan, the Nambu series of automatics (named for Colonel Nambu Kirijo, the nation's foremost weapons designer), chambered for 8mm, came into use. The Walther P38 gradually replaced the Luger in the Wehrmacht (German Army) during World War II.

CZ27 AUTO

A refinement of a German design, the Ceska Zbrojovoka Model 1927 (CZ27) was a straight blowback-operated 9mm with a 9-round magazine. Following its occupation of Czechoslovakia, Germany diverted the production of that nation's excellent arms industry, including Ceska Zbrojovoka, for its own use.

NAMBU M94

Many firearms experts consider the notorious Japanese Nambu Type 94 automatic to be the worst military pistol of modern times. The cocking mechanism was so poorly designed that the weapon could fire accidentally if any pressure was put on it. In addition, the majority of these pistols were manufactured toward the end World War II, when Allied bombing was battering Japan's arms industries, so materials and workmanship were particularly poor.

NAMBU M14

The Nambu Type 14 was so-called because it was first produced in 1925, the fourteenth year in the reign of the Emperor Yoshito—a naming convention used for some other Japanese military weapons. The 8mm automatic was the principal Japanese military pistol of World War II, but because Japanese officers were required to personally purchase their sidearms, a variety of pistols saw service.

LUGER WITH DRUM MAGAZINE

Although the Walther P38 largely replaced the Luger as the standard German service pistol, the latter still saw much service in World War II. This particular pistol—fitted with a 32-round drum magazine—was taken from a German general following the Allied capture of the North African city of Tunis in May 1943. The so-called "snail drum" magazine was never popular because it had a tendency to jam.

WALTHER P38

A military adaptation of the PP (Polizei Pistole, or Police Pistol) series of pistols developed by Carl Walther Waffenfabrik in the 1920s, the 9mm P38 was adopted by the German Wehrmacht in the 1930s to replace the more expensive and complicated Luger. The P38's action was designed so that as long as the safety was on, it could be carried while cocked and ready to fire when the safety was disengaged—a highly desirable feature in a service pistol.

BERETTA M1934 AUTO

The blowback-operated 9mm Beretta M1934 was Italy's standard sidearm in its wars in Africa in the 1930s and in World War II. The M1934 was mainly army-issue; a 7.65mm version, the M1935, was used principally by the Italian navy and air force.

THE HOUSE OF BERETTA

In 1526 the Venetian Republic contracted with gunsmith Bartoleomo Beretta of Gardone for a quantity of arquebuses. That deal was the start of a gunmaking dynasty that has endured for nearly half a millennium; the modern firm of Fabbrica d'Armi Pietro Beretta is still largely owned and run by Bartolemo's descendants. The firm's reputation for high quality and excellence in design has made it one of the world's foremost manufacturers of weapons for both military, police, and sporting use. While it makes every kind of gun from shotguns to assault rifles, Beretta's pistols are held in especially high regard. This was dramatically underscored by the U.S. Army's 1985 adoption of the 9mm Beretta M92SB/92F as its standard sidearm, replacing the venerable Colt .45 M1911.

Allied Pistols

U.S. forces continued to carry the Colt M1911—and would do so for four decades after the war's end. The British, however, retained their great devotion to Webley revolvers in World War II, although quantities of the Browning High Power 9mm automatic (see p 87, image p 6) were issued to British forces.

WEBLEY MARK IV
Introduced in 1899, the Webley Mark IV revolver remained popular with British forces—especially the aircrew of the Royal Air Force—during World War II. Originally .455, World War II–era Mark IV's were more commonly of .38 caliber. The pistol here is shown in subdued "wartime" finish.

WEBLEY MARK VI
This variant of the Webley Mark VI (introduced in 1916) is chambered for the .22 round and fitted with a special cylinder. It was used to train British troops in pistol shooting during World War II. (The use of the .22 cartridge allowed firing on relatively compact shooting ranges.)

SWEDISH M40 PISTOL

When the outbreak of World War II led Germany to suspend export of the Walther HP pistol, which neutral Sweden had just adopted as its service pistol, the Swedish government licensed a 1935 design from Finnish designer Almo Lahti. The 9mm M40, as it was known in Swedish service, looked like a Luger but used a firing system closer to that of a Bergmann-Bayard, with an added kick to ensure proper action movement in cold temperatures.

TOKAREV

Developed by Feodor Tokarev, a former Czarist officer turned Soviet gun designer, the Tokarev pistol was introduced in the late 1920s and adopted as the standard Red Army sidearm a few years later. Known as the TT (from "Tula-Tokarev," Tula being one of the principal Soviet arsenals), the pistol's firing system was essentially a copy of the one used in John Browning's Colt M1911 .45, chambered for the 7.62 round. The original model, the TT30, was later replaced by the TT-33 (shown here).

WEBLEY 7.65 AUTO

While Webley & Scott was best known for revolvers, it produced several fine automatics over the years. This 7.65mm model was one of fifty especially made for the City of London Police (who traditionally do not carry firearms) for use in case of invasion during the dark days of 1939–41, when Britain fought Nazi Germany virtually alone.

World War II Rifles

When World War II broke out only one nation, the U.S., had adopted a semiautomatic rifle—the M1 Garand (see sidebar)—as its standard infantry arm. The tempo of rifle design quickened, however, when the militaries of other nations realized that in modern warfare, a high rate of fire at short range was often more important than long-range accuracy.

In 1942, Germany developed the 7.92mm Fallschirmgewehr (Paratroop rifle) for its airborne forces, which could fire in both single-shot and fully automatic modes. Two years later came the MP44, another 7.92 selective-fire weapon meant to combine the functions of the rifle, submachine gun, and light machine gun. A truly revolutionary gun, the MP44's alternate designation, Sturmgewehr, would provide the name for an entirely new class of weapon—the assault rifle.

M1 CARBINE

In the run-up to World War II, the U.S. decided to develop an "intermediate" weapon for use by officers and NCOs, armored crews, truck drivers, and support personnel—one that would be more compact than the M1 Garand rifle but more effective in combat than the M1911 pistol. The result was the M1 carbine, a lightweight (5.5lb/25kg), semiautomatic weapon firing a special .30 cartridge. The M1 was followed by the M2, which was capable of full-auto as well as semi-auto fire, and a folding-stock version of the M1 (the M1A1, shown here) was developed for airborne troops. Although more than 6 million such carbines were issued before production ceased in the 1950s, the combat verdict was mixed; the weapon proved handy in street fighting in Europe and in jungle fighting in the Pacific, but many thought that it was too delicate and that the pistol-strength .30 carbine cartridge was too weak.

JAPANESE TYPE 38

Introduced in 1905—the thirty-eigth year of the Emperor Meiji's reign, and thus named the Type 38—this 6.5 bolt-action rifle was the standard Japanese service rifle until the introduction of the Type 99 thirty-four years later. It was also produced in a carbine version.

JAPANESE TYPE 99 RIFLE

Firing a more powerful round (7.7mm) than the earlier 6.5 Type 38 Arisaka rifle, the Japanese Type 99 rifle first entered service in 1939. The Type 99's most distinctive features are an integral wire monopod and a set of rear sights that (very optimistically) were intended for use against aircraft.

JOHN C. GARAND

Born in Quebec in 1888, John Cantius Garand (pictured at left) moved, as a child, to New England with his family, where he worked in textile mills and machine shops. His passion was for weapons design, however, and during World War I he submitted a design for a light machine gun to the U.S. Army. It was adopted, but put into production too late to see service. His obvious talents led to a position as an engineer with the U.S. government arsenal at Springfield, Massachusetts.

There, in the early 1930s, he developed a gas-operated, 8-shot, .30 semiautomatic rifle that beat out competitors to win adoption by the U.S. Army in 1936. (The Marine Corps also adopted the rifle, but shortages led the marines to fight their first battles of World War II with bolt-action M1903 Springfields.) The M1 Garand gave U.S. forces a big advantage in firepower during that conflict; General George S. Patton described the rifle as "the greatest battle implement ever devised."

The M1 Garand remained the standard U.S. infantry weapon through the Korean War (1950–53), and the rifle that replaced it in the mid–1950s, the M14, was essentially a selective-fire version of the M1. As a government employee, Garand earned no royalties on his design, though almost 6 million were eventually produced. A resolution to grant Garand a special bonus of $100,000 failed to pass Congress. He died in Massachusetts in 1974.

1169 ENTRENCHING TOOL BAYONET (BRITISH)
Issued to British troops in World War II, this entrenching tool combined a spade and a pick for digging foxholes; with a spike bayonet fixed to the handle, it could be used to probe for land mines.

M1 GARAND
Despite its undoubted success on the battlefield, the M1 Garand was not without its drawbacks. The rifle's magazine fed only from an eight-round stripper clip, so in combat it could not be topped off by inserting individual rounds into the magazine. And when the clip was emptied, it was ejected upward with a distinctive clang! sound that could betray the firer's location to the enemy.

MANNLICHER-CARCANO CARBINE/GRENADE LAUNCHER
A true rarity from World War II, this weapon was a combination 6-shot carbine and grenade launcher. While most infantry rifles of the World Wars era could fire grenades from a cup fitted into the barrel, the gun had a permanently attached grenade launcher on its right side.

Machine Guns of World War II

Besides their infantry application, World War I also saw machine guns fitted to aircraft (and used against them from the ground), armored cars, and tanks. In the interwar years, weapons designers developed even more powerful machine guns, like John Browning's .50 M2, which fired a cartridge the size of an old-fashioned Coca-Cola bottle. Even before World War I ended, however, several nations sought to package the punch of the machine   gun in a weapon that could be carried by an individual infantryman.

By World War II, these included the British Bren gun and the U.S. BAR (Browning Automatic Rifle). These weapons were typically magazine-fed, but based on their experience in World War I, the German Wehrmacht made a belt-fed light machine gun, the 7.92mm MG42, the foundation of its infantry squad in World War II. The concept of the "squad automatic weapon" evolved, postwar, into guns like the U.S. military's Vietnam-era M60 and the contemporary M249, the latter based on a Belgian design.

JAPANESE AIRCRAFT CANNON
While the British Royal Air Force (RAF) and the U.S. Army Air Forces (USAAF) armed their fighters and bombers mostly with machine guns, the air forces of other nations preferred automatic cannons, usually 20mm weapons firing explosive shells rather than bullets. Such as this 20mm Japanese aircraft cannon.

GERMAN MG42
One of World War II's most effective weapons, the 7.92mm, belt-fed German MG34 and its wartime replacement, the MG42, were distinguished by their versatility. Equipped with a bipod, they went into action in an infantry support role. Tripod-mounted, they proved an excellent defensive weapon; and they could be fitted on tanks and other vehicles as well. The MG series' high rate of fire—up to 1200 rounds per minute—and their distinctive sound led Allied troops to nickname the weapon "Hitler's Zipper."

BROWNING M2

During World War I, John Browning designed the .30 machine gun shown here for aircraft use; designated the M2, it didn't arrive in time to see wartime service. The weapon was used by the U.S. Army Air Corps (later the U.S. Army Air Forces) into the early days of World War II, when it was largely replaced by the formidable .50 M2.

BROWNING AUTOMATIC RIFLE

Another Browning design, the gas-operated, .30 Browning Automatic Rifle (BAR) was introduced in 1918, too late to see more than limited service in World War I. It would remain in U.S. service, with some modifications, through the Korean War (1950–53). In most respects an excellent weapon, capable of both fully automatic fire and, in the hands of an experienced user, single shots. Disadvantages included its weight (19.5lb/8.9kg) and its magazine capacity of only 20 rounds—low for a full-auto weapon.

"Why does the soul always require a machine-gun?"

—E.M. Foster, from "What Has Germany Done to the Germans?" 1940

Submachine Guns of World War II

As World War I ground to a bloody stalemate on the Western Front, soldiers of the warring nations began to acknowledge the inadequacies of the standard infantry rifle—its length, weight, and above all its relatively slow rate of fire. As a result—and inspired by the success of the machine gun (see pp 114–15, 132–33)—weapons designers developed the submachine gun. This infantryman's firearm sacrificed the rifle's long-range accuracy in favor of a smaller weapon that could be fired from the hip or shoulder, and which could unleash a rapid volume of fire in close combat. Refined in the interwar years, the submachine gun figured prominently in World War II, and even today—when the assault rifle has largely subsumed its functions—submachine guns retain a role in antiterrorism and other specialized operations.

THE SUBMACHINE GUN'S ORIGINS
The Italian Army introduced a prototypical submachine gun in 1915, but pride of place in the weapon's development really goes to Germany, which, three years later, adopted the Bergmann MP18/1 designed by Hugo Schmeisser. The blowback-operated weapon fired a slightly modified version of the 9mm parabellum round used in the Luger pistol. The MP18/1 originally used the 32-round "snail drum" magazine also developed for the Luger, but postwar versions used a side-mounted box magazine. The MP18/1 arrived too late and in too few numbers to change Germany's fortunes on the Western Front. Around the same time

the Bergmann was being developed, U.S. Army colonel J.T. Thompson designed the now-legendary gun that bears his name but by the time the first Thompsons were ready for shipping, the Armistice had been signed.

WORLD WAR II AND AFTER
Most nations adopted some form of submachine gun before the advent of World War II, although military conservatives often derided the weapon as "cheap and nasty" and lamented its relative lack of accuracy and "stopping power" (most submachine guns fired a pistol-strength cartridge rather than a rifle round, the latter being too powerful for the submachine gun's firing system.)

The weapon proved its worth, however, in all theaters of World War II, especially in street-fighting in Europe and in close-quarter battle in the Pacific islands.

The Soviet Union especially took to the weapon, producing millions of PPSh41/42/43 models, and even equipping whole battalions with them. While technically crude compared to German submachine guns like the MP40, the PPSh series (short for *Pistolet Pullemet Sh*pagin) were rugged and reliable in the brutal conditions of the Eastern Front, easy to use even by minimally trained Red Army soldiers, and could be produced quickly and cheaply. Chinese copies of the Russian design, like the Type 50, saw extensive service in the Korean War (1950–53), in which U.S. troops dubbed them "burp guns" from their distinctive sound.

STEN
Simple and cheap to manufacture and easy to use, the STEN submachine gun and its numerous variants were a mainstay of British and Commonwealth forces throughout World War II. Its name derived from the initials of its designers, R.V. Shepard and H.J. Turpin, combined with those of Britain's Enfield National Arsenal. The 9mm, blowback-operated submachine gun—which fed from a 32-round, side-mounted detachable magazine—saw service everywhere from Normandy to New Guinea. The Australian version was known as the AUSTEN, from "Australian STEN."

FRENCH MAS

The 7.65mm MAS (from Manufacture d'Armes de St. Etienne) Model 1938 submachine gun was the French army's principal World War II sub-machine gun. It was an unusual weapon in that the trigger had to be pushed forward to put the weapon in safety mode and the bolt recoiled into a tube inside the buttstock.

REISING

The U.S. .45 Reising gun (named for its designer, Eugene Reising) was a selective-fire, delayed blowback-operation weapon used by the U.S. Marine Corps early in World War II. Issued in a full-length, wooden-stock version as well as the folding wire-stock model shown here, the Reising's locked-breech firing system was susceptible to fouling from dirt and moisture, so it proved ineffective and unpopular in the jungle campaigns on Guadalcanal and other islands.

MP40

Although popularly known as the "Schmeisser," this German submachine gun, officially the MP (Machinenpistole) Model 1940, was not in fact developed by the great German weapons designer Hugo Schmeisser. More than 1 million were manufactured for Wehrmacht use during World War II, and the 9mm, blowback-operated, metal-and-plastic MP40 is generally considered the first standard-issue infantry weapon to use no wood in its construction. Its excellent reputation is reinforced by the fact that many Allied troops used captured MP40s in preference to their own issue submachine guns.

MP44

Officially the MP (Machinenpistole) Model 1944, aka the Sturmgewehr (Assault Rifle) Model 1944, this gun represented the cutting edge of small-arms technology as World War II headed to its bloody close. Gas-operated, the selective-fire weapon used a short (kurtz) version of the standard 7.92 German cartridge, feeding from a detachable 30-round magazine. (Although designated "44," the first models were issued in 1943.) The Soviet AK-47 design (see p 140), the world's most popular assault rifle, is a direct descendant. The MP44 shown here was issued with a special curved barrel—useful for shooting around corners in street fighting.

Specialized Weapons of World War II

The special battlefield conditions of World War II required specialized infantry weapons. The appearance of the tank as a major battlefield presence led to the development of rocket-propelled weapons to allow infantrymen to deal with enemy armor. In the brutal conflict between the Soviet Union and Nazi Germany on the Eastern Front, both armies fielded sniper units armed with specially adapted rifles. While World War II saw the widespread use of radios for communication, the venerable flare pistol continued to be used for signaling when radio silence had to be observed. A grimmer type of weapon were the brutal devices used in Nazi Germany's POW and concentration camps.

SNIPERS

Many World War II armies made use of snipers to kill at long ranges. Most of these shooters used conventional bolt-action service rifles or civilian hunting rifles fitted with telescopic scopes. The Soviet Red Army especially took to sniping; the "highest-scoring" snipers (some of them women) became national celebrities. The most famous Soviet sniper, Vasily Grigoryevich Zaitsev (1915–1991), had 225 confirmed kills. During the Battle of Stalingrad, Zaitsev reportedly killed one of the Wehrmacht's top snipers, who had been sent to the city specifically to hunt Zaitsev down. This duel was the basis for David L. Robbins's 1999 novel *War of the Rats* and the 2001 movie *Enemy at the Gates*. Zaitsev and his fellow snipers used the standard Mosin-Nagant (see p 113), which remained in service in the Soviet Union and its satellites until the 1960s.

ANTI-TANK WEAPONS

During World War I and in the interwar years, the principal antitank weapon was the antitank rifle—high-powered weapons firing heavy, armor-piercing rounds. The best-known weapons of this type are the British Army's .55 Boys and the German 13.2mm Mauser Panzerbusche. As tank armor was made thicker after the outbreak of World War II, antitank rifles proved increasingly ineffective. The U.S. Army was the first to develop a rocket-powered antitank weapon. Introduced in 1942, the M1A1 "Bazooka" was a shoulder-mounted tube, operated by a two-man team, that fired a 2.36in/60mm HEAT (High Explosive Anti-Tank) projectile. (The Bazooka got its nickname because it looked like a spoof musical instrument played by a popular comedian.) The Germans copied the weapon—upgrading its caliber to 3.5in/88mm—as the Panzerschreck. The Wehrmacht also used large numbers of a simple, one-shot rocket-launcher, the Panzerfaust, while the British Army adopted the rather unique PIAT.

GERMAN SNIPER RIFLE

During World War II, the German Wehrmacht adapted pre-war Mauser rifles, made originally as civilian hunting and target weapons, for use by snipers. The 8mm Mauser shown here is fitted with a Hensolt single-post telescopic sight. An American officer took this particular rifle from a dead German sniper during the Battle of the Bulge in the winter of 1944–45.

GERMAN FLARE PISTOL

Made of zinc, this World War II Walther German flare pistol (leuchtpistol) could fire both flares or tear-gas cartridges. The breech opens by means of a downward pull on the trigger guard.

DOUBLE-BARREL GERMAN FLARE PISTOL

Flares were used not only for signaling on the ground, but also from the air—for example, to alert ground crews to be prepared for on-board casualties before landing, or to indicate changes in formation while in flight. Shown here is a double-barreled flare pistol used by the Luftwaffe, Nazi Germany's air force. A "hammerless" design, the weapon cocks when broken open for loading, applying the safety automatically when the barrels return to firing position.

PIAT

First used in combat in 1943, the British Army's PIAT (Personal Infantry Anti-Tank Projector) was an unusual weapon in that it used a spring-loaded firing system to ignite a relatively small propulsion charge, which in turn sent a HEAT (High-Explosive Anti-Tank) round to a maximum of 330ft/100m. The PIAT's advantage was that, unlike the U.S. bazooka, it did not spew a sheet of flame upon firing, revealing the user's position to the enemy. For the same reason, the PIAT was safe to use in tight spaces in a non-antitank role—house-to-house fighting, for example. Its disadvantages were its heavy weight (34lb/15kg) and the inability of the 3lb/1.4kg HEAT round to penetrate the frontal armor of some German panzer (tank) models.

Weapons of Espionage

Some of the most innovative and intriguing weapons are those intended for use by spies, assassins, intelligence agents, and guerrilla fighters. Because concealment is obviously of paramount importance for their users, many of these weapons (including most of the items shown on these pages) are disguised as ordinary objects. While some specialized espionage weapons were made in the nineteenth and early twentieth centuries, their real heyday was during World War II and the decades of Cold War that followed.

OSS AND SOE

In June 1942, six months after its entry into World War II, the United States set up the Office of Strategic Services (OSS), an agency whose missions included not only gathering intelligence, but carrying out sabotage and aiding resistance movements in areas occupied by the Axis powers (Germany, Italy, and Japan), in close cooperation with its British counterpart, the Special Operations Executive (SOE).

Drawing many of its operatives from Ivy League universities and other bastions of the East Coast "establishment" (detractors claimed its initials stood for "Oh So Social"), the OSS used a variety of unusual weapons in its clandestine operations, many developed by the National Defense Resource Council (NDRC), like the famous "Liberator" single-shot pistol (see sidebar), or borrowed from the British, like the Sykes-Fairbairn Commando Knife.

THE COLD WAR

When World War II gave way to the Cold War, the OSS gave way to the Central Intelligence Agency (CIA). The CIA continued the use of one the most effective OSS weapons, the .22 Hi-Standard automatic pistol. With a design similar to the civilian Colt Woodsmen pistol, the Hi-Standard was equipped with a silencer developed by Bell Telephone Laboratories. In keeping with the agency's doctrine of "plausible deniability" in covert operations, the Hi-Standards in the CIA's arsenal were manufactured without any markings that would indicate their American origin. The CIA also developed its share of unusual weapons; reportedly, the agency worked up an exploding seashell in an unsuccessful effort to kill Cuban dictator Fidel Castro, an avid skin-diver.

The KGB, the postwar version of the Soviet Secret Police, had its own arsenal of unusual weapons, including a 4.5mm gun disguised as a lipstick (issued to female agents, it was nicknamed "the Kiss of Death"); an umbrella firing poison pellets, used to assassinate Bulgarian dissident Georgi Malenkov in London in 1978; and perhaps most bizarre, the "rektal" knife—a dagger designed to be concealed in that particular body cavity.

GAS GUN
Patented in 1932 as a "disabling gas firing weapon" by the Lake Erie Chemical Corporation of Ohio, this pen-shaped device was designed to discharge tear gas. Although intended for use by law-enforcement agencies, similar devices discharging more deadly chemical compounds have been used in espionage by various secret services.

DART AND DAGGER
Two OSS/SOE weapons of World War II: The dart (above) could be fired by a pistol-style crossbow using rubber bands, while the easily concealable wrist dagger was widely issued to Allied operatives.

MIGHTIER THAN THE SWORD
This German pen gun from World War II fired a .22 round. The weapon was cocked by pulling back on the top and fired by pressing a small button on the side.

LOZENGE-CASE GUN

An agent of Italy's Fascist government reportedly used this pistol, disguised as a tin of throat lozenges, to assassinate an American intelligence operative in Switzerland during World War II. (As a neutral nation, Switzerland was a hotbed of espionage and intrigue throughout the conflict.) To fire the weapon, the assassin opened the lid and pressed on one of the "lozenges," which served as a trigger.

DEADLY TOOLS

The tire gauge and screwdriver shown here are replicas of actual weapons produced for Allied operatives in World War II. Each is a single-shot .22 pistol.

DEADLY MUSIC

Made in 1965, this fully functional silver flute was adapted to fire a .22 round. A brass screw on one of the keys functions as a trigger.

THE LIBERATOR

Although not produced especially for the OSS, the "Liberator" pistol has—rightly or wrongly—long been associated with that organization. The Liberator was simplicity itself: A single-shot pistol firing a .45 ACP round through a smoothbore barrel. Made of 23 pieces of stamped metal, it came in a cardboard box with ten cartridges (five of which could be stored in a compartment in the grip), a wooden rod for ejecting spent cartridges, and wordless, comic strip-style sheet with assembly instructions. About a million of these guns were made by the Guide Lamp Division of the General Motors Corporation in 1942. The weapon was nicknamed "the Woolworth gun" after the discount store where all items sold for five or ten cents. (The actual unit cost was about U.S. $2.00.)

With an effective range of about six feet, the Liberator was really a weapon designed to allow the user (if he or she were brave and lucky) to obtain better weapons. This gun was apparently intended for mass distribution to resistance fighters in Axis-occupied Europe and Asia, the idea being that they would be used on stragglers and sentries, whose weapons would then be captured and added to the guerrilla group's arsenal.

Just how many Liberators actually saw service, and where, and how effectively are questions fiercely debated by firearms historians. While they may have been originally intended mainly for distribution in Nazi-occupied Europe, there's not much evidence many were actually used there, but guerrillas fighting Japanese forces in the Philippines apparently used some Liberators to good effect.

In the early 1960s, the CIA revived the idea of a no-frills, single-shot pistol in the form of the so-called "deer gun," a 9mm weapon the U.S. distributed to anticommunist guerillas in Southeast Asia.

Post–World War II Weapons

The most significant development in firearms in the decades after World War II was the incredible proliferation of the assault rifle, especially the AK47. Critics have charged that the widespread availability of these cheap but deadly weapons fuels ongoing civil, political, and ethnic conflict in the world's poorest regions, such as sub-Saharan Africa. Recent decades have seen civilian and military engineers experimenting with "caseless" ammunition and even rocket propulsion to replace conventional ammunition and firing systems, but most contemporary firearms remain based (albeit in highly evolved forms) on designs and systems introduced decades ago or even in the nineteenth century. As the events of September 11, 2001, showed, in the twenty-first century, even the simplest weapons—box-cutters and ceramic knifes—can still be used to devastating effect.

INFANTRY WEAPONS

The most successful infantry weapon of the post–World War II era is the AK47 assault rifle, often called the Kalashnikov after its chief designer (see sidebar). Simple construction with few moving parts made this rifle easy to maintain and use even by relatively untrained troops or guerrilla fighters. The AK47 remains ubiquitous in the twenty-first century, with as many as 100 million of the weapon and its variants produced as of this writing.

The postwar years saw the armies of most nations adopt selective-fire assault rifles, most (like the Belgian FN FAL, introduced in 1950 and adopted by more than 50 nations) chambered for the 7.62mm round. An exception was the U.S., which adopted the 5.56mm M16, based on the Armalite rifle designed by Eugene Stoner, in the mid-1960s. In recent years, many armies have adopted rifles using smaller cartridges, often in "bullpup" designs that place the magazine and action behind the trigger guard. Just as the assault rifle was an outgrowth of the World War II German Sturmgewehr (see pp 130–31), the belt-fed squad automatic weapons now used by many armies are an evolution of the German MG42 (see p 132).

HANDGUNS

Pistol design lagged somewhat until the 1970s, when the rise of terrorism led to the development of a new generation of automatics, most chambered for 9mm. Intended to meet the needs of law-enforcement agencies and antiterrorist military units, these pistols could be carried safely, used in close confines (like airplane passenger cabins) with minimal danger to hostages or bystanders, and had a high magazine capacity.

One of the first pistols to meet these criteria was Germany's Heckler & Koch VP70, also the first pistol made with plastic in its construction. In 1983 the Austrian firm Glock AG introduced the first of its extremely successful Glock series of automatics, with magazine capacities of up to 19 rounds. Glocks are composed mostly of plastic, which led to fears they could pass through metal detectors, but these fears have proven unfounded.

AK47
Perhaps the AK47's greatest virtue is its reliability under tough combat conditions: During the Vietnam War, Vietcong guerrillas reportedly retrieved AK47s hidden for days in muddy rice paddies, but which fired perfectly. In contrast, the U.S. M16—while a technically superior and, in some respects, more lethal rifle—has to be kept meticulously clean to avoid jamming. The model shown here is a Chinese version.

WESTON MINIATURE

Although Tom Weston is perhaps the best-known twentieth-century maker of miniature guns, the details of his life are sketchy. The Mexico City resident was apparently a leading collector and seller of antique firearms when, in the 1930s, he engaged Mexican craftsmen to make tiny but fully functioning guns. These unique weapons, produced mainly in the 1950s and 1960s, are prized by collectors of firearms curiosa. Shown here is a 2mm "Reforma" single-shot pistol.

GYROJET PISTOL

Americans Robert Mainhardt and Art Biehl developed one of the most unusual and innovative firearms of recent decades, the Gyrojet pistol, in the early 1960s. The Gyrojet was actually a pistol-scale rocket launcher, firing a 12mm (later 13mm) projectile burning a solid propellant. MBA Associates, the company Mainhardt and Biehl set up to manufacture the weapon, also produced a carbine version. According to some sources, the U.S. military became interested in the Gyrojet concept because it seemed to promise a "jam-free," recoilless infantry weapon, but it proved impractical in tests under combat conditions. Gyrojet weapons never found much of a civilian buyership because of the expensive ammunition.

M. T. KALASHNIKOV

Born in Kurya, Siberia, in 1919, Mikhail Timofeyevich Kalashnikov had no formal technical education, instead, receiving hands-on training as a railway "technical clerk." Seriously wounded in 1941 while serving as a tank commander with the Red Army, Kalashnikov began working on weapons designs during his convalescence. He designed a couple of submachine guns, but as the Red Army already had successful submachine guns in production (see pp 134–35), they weren't adopted. Kalashnikov then turned his talents toward the development of a weapon known, in Soviet terminology, as an "Automat"—the same assault-rifle concept pioneered by the Germans with the MP44 (see p 135). (The German weapons designer Hugo Schmeisser and some of his associates, who had been captured and pressed into Soviet service at the end of World War II, may have contributed to Kalashnikov's work; this is still debated.) In 1947 the Automat Kalashnikov (AK) Model 47, debuted, and the Red Army adopted the weapon in 1951. Kalashnikov rose to the post of chief weapons designer for the Soviet military, produced other weapons (such as the 5.54mm AK-74), won every award possible in the Soviet Union and, later, the Russian Federation. In 2004, he endorsed his own brand of vodka. He is still alive at this writing.

WINCHESTER MODEL 70
Produced in a variety of calibers (from .22 to .458 magnum) and configurations from 1936 to the present day, the bolt-action Winchester Model 70 is considered one of the finest sporting rifles of all times.

SKS CARBINE
During World War II, Soviet weapons designer Sergei Simonov worked to develop a semiautomatic rifle firing a "short" version of the standard 7.62mm Soviet round. The result was the SKS-45 carbine, a gas-operated weapon that fed from a 10-round box magazine and featured an integral bayonet that folded into the forestock. The SKS was a highly successful weapon and it was produced in large numbers in China and other nations until it was largely replaced by the AK47.

AK47
Perhaps the AK47's greatest virtue is it's reliability under tough combat conditions: During the Vietnam War, Vietcong guerillas reportedly retrieved AK47shidden for days in muddy rice paddies, but which fired perfectly.

Bibliography

Agoston, Gabor, and David Morgan. *Guns for the Sultan: Military Power and the Weapons Industry in the Ottoman Empire.* New York: Cambridge University Press, 2005.

Ahearn, Bill. *Muskets of the Revolution and the French & Indian Wars.* Woonsocket, RI: Andrew Mowbray Publications, 2005.

Akehurst, Richard. *The World of Guns.* London: Hamlyn, 1972.

Anglim, Simon, et al. *Fighting Techniques of the Ancient World (3000 B.C. to A.D. 500): Equipment, Combat Skills, and Tactics.* New York: Thomas Dunne Books, 2003.

Armour, Richard. *It All Started with Stones and Clubs: Being a Short History of War and Weaponry from Earliest Times to the Present, Noting the Gratifying Progress Made by Man Since His First Crude, Small-Scale Efforts to Do Away with Those Who Disagreed with Him.* New York: McGraw-Hill, 1967.

Berk, Joseph. *Gatling Gun: 19th-century Machine Gun to 21st-century Vulcan.* Boulder, CO: Paladin Press, 1991.

Bezdek, Richard H. *American Swords and Sword Makers.* Boulder, CO: Paladin Press, 1994.

Blackmore, Howard L. *Hunting Weapons: From the Middle Ages to the Twentieth Century.* Mineola, NY: Dover Publications, 2000.

Boorman, Dean K. *History of Winchester Firearms.* Guilford, CT: The Lyons Press, 2001.

Breuer, William B. *Secret Weapons of World War II.* New York: Wiley, 2002.

Bruce, Robert. *German Automatic Weapons of World War II.* Marlborough, UK: Crowood Press, 1998.

Canby, Courtlandt. *A History of Weaponry.* New York: Hawthorne Books, 1963.

Canfield, Bruce N. *U.S. Infantry Weapons of World War II.* Woonsocket, RI: Andrew Mowbray Publications, 1996.

Chapel, Charles Edward. *The Gun Collector's Handbook of Values* (eighth rev. ed.). New York: Coward-McCann, 1968.

Collier, James Lincoln. *Gunpowder and Weaponry.* New York: Benchmark Books, 2004.

Finnish mortar

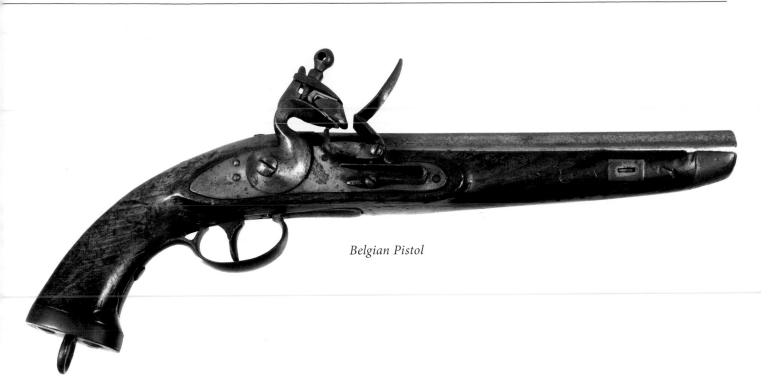

Belgian Pistol

Craig, Philip. *The World's Great Small Arms*. London: Amber Books, 1993.

Daugherty III, Leo. *Fighting Techniques of a Japanese Infantryman 1941–1945: Training, Techniques and Weapons*. Staplehurst, UK: Spellmount Publishers, 2002.

David, Nicolle. *Mughul India 1504–1761*. Oxford, UK: Osprey, 1993.

Diagram Group. *Weapons: An International Encyclopedia from 5000 B.C. to A.D. 2000*. New York: St. Martin's Griffin, 1991.

Draeger, Donn F. *The Weapons and Fighting Arts of Indonesia*. North Clarendon, VT: Tuttle Publishing, 2001.

Dupur, Tervor Nevitt. *The Evolution of Weapons and Warfare*. Cambridge, MA: Da Capo Press, 1990.

Fleming, David. *Weapons of the Waffen SS*. St. Paul, MN: MBI Publishing Company, 2003.

Gommans, Joseph. *Mughal Warfare: Indian Frontiers and Highroads to Empire 1500–1700*. New York: Routledge, 2003.

Hall, Bert S. *Weapons and Warfare in Renaissance Europe: Gunpowder, Technology, and Tactics*. Baltimore, MD: Johns Hopkins University Press, 2001.

Healy, Mark, and Angus McBride. *The Ancient Assyrians*. Oxford, UK: Osprey, 1992.

Hogg, Ian. *The Guinness Encyclopedia of Weaponry*. Enfield, Middlesex, UK: Guinness Publishing, 1992.

———. *Handguns & Rifles: The Finest Weapons from Around the World*. Guilford, CT: The Lyons Press, 2003.

Hogg, Ian, and John Walter. *Pistols of the World* (fourth ed.). Iola, WI: Krause Publications, 2004.

Hogg, Ian, and John Weeks. *Military Small Arms of the 20th Century* (seventh ed.) Iola, WI: Krause Publications, 2000.

Holmes, Richard. *Britain at War: Famous British Battles from Hastings to Normandy, 1066–1944.* Irvington, NY: Hylas Publishing, 2004.

Hutton, Alfred. *The Sword and the Centuries.* Boulder, CO: Paladin Press, 2002.

Izuka, Kunio. *Weapons of the Samurai.* London: Chrysalis Books, 2001.

Kelly, Jack. *Gunpowder: Alchemy, Bombards, and Pyrotechnics—The History of the Explosive That Changed the World.* New York: Basic Books, 2004.

Kern, Paul Bentley. *Ancient Siege Warfare.* Indianapolis: Indiana University Press, 1999.

Marcot, Roy. *The History of Remington Firearms: The History of One of the World's Most Famous Gun Makers.* Guilford, CT: The Lyons Press, 2005.

McChristian, Douglas C. *The U.S. Army in the West, 1870–1880: Uniforms, Weapons, and Equipment.* Oklahoma City: University of Oklahoma Press, 2000.

McNab, Chris. *The Great Book of Guns: An Illustrated History of Military, Sporting, and Antique Firearms.* San Diego, CA: Thunder Bay Press, 2004.

Medieval Siege Weapons: Western Europe AD 585–1385. Oxford, UK: Osprey, 2002.

Miller, David, ed. *The Illustrated Book of Guns.* London: Salamander Books, 2000.

———, ed. *Illustrated Directory of Twentieth-Century Guns.* St. Paul, MN: MBI Publishing Company, 2003.

Nagayama, Kokan. *The Connoisseur's Book of Japanese Swords.* Translated from the Japanese by Kenji Mishina. Tokyo: Kodansha International, 1998.

Nicholson, Helen. *Medieval Warfare.* New York: Palgrave Macmillan, 2004.

Nicolle, David, and Christa Hook. *Italian Militiaman 1260–1392.* Oxford, UK: Osprey, 1999.

O'Connell, Richard, and John Batchelor. *Soul of the Sword: An Illustrated History of Weaponry and Warfare from Prehistory to the Present.* New York: Free Press, 2002.

Partridge, Robert B. *Fighting Pharaohs: Weapons and Warfare in Ancient Egypt.* Clearwater, FL: Peartree Books, 2002.

Poyer, Joe. *U.S. Winchester Trench and Riot Guns and Other U.S. Combat Shotguns: For Collectors Only.* Tustin, CA: North Cape Publications, 1992.

Pritchard Jr., Russ A. *Civil War Weapons and Equipment.* Guilford, CT: The Lyons Press, 2003.

Pyhrr, Stuart W., Donald J. LoRocca, and Morihiro Ogawa. *Arms and Armor: Notable Acquisitions 1991–2002.* New York: Metropolitan Museum of Art, 2003.

Ricketts, Howard. *Firearms*. London: Octopus Books, 1972.

Sato, Kanzan. *The Japanese Sword: A Comprehensive Guide*. Translated from the Japanese by Joe Earle. Tokyo: Kodansha America, 1983.

Stratton, Charles R. *British Enfield Rifles, Vol. 4, the Pattern 1914 and U.S. Model 1917 Enfield Rifles*. Tustin, CA: North Cape Publications, 2000.

Thompson, Logan. *Ancient Weapons in Britain*. South Yorkshire, UK: Pen and Sword, 2005.

Tunis, Edwin. *Weapons: A Pictorial History*. Baltimore, MD: The Johns Hopkins University Press, 1999.

Turnbull, Stephen, and Wayne Reynolds. *Siege Weapons of the Far East: AD 960–1644*. Oxford, UK: Osprey, 2002.

Van Zonneveld, Albert G. *Traditional Weapons of the Indonesian Archipelago*. Amsterdam: KITLV Press (Royal Netherlands Academy of Arts and Sciences), 2002.

Walter, John. *The Luger Story: The Standard History of the World's Most Famous Handgun*. London: Greenhill Books, 2001.

Warry, John Gibson. *Warfare in the Classical World: An Illustrated Encyclopedia of Weapons, Warriors, and Warfare in the Ancient Civilizations of Greece and Rome*. New York: St. Martin's Press, 1981.

Watts, Steven. *Practicing Primitive: A Handbook of Aboriginal Skills*. Layton, Utah: Gibbs Smith, 2005.

Weir, William. *Fifty Weapons That Changed Warfare*. Franklin Lakes, NJ: New Page Books, 2005.

Mitrailleuse

Acknowledgments

Unless otherwise noted, all silhouetted weaponry images are from the Berman Museum of World History, Anniston, Alabama, with the exception of the following:

Colt Peacemaker © 2006 Jupiterimages Corporation;

Model 1911 Colt Semi-Automatic © 2006 Jupiterimages Corporation;

Broomhandle Mauser © 2006 Jupiterimages Corporation;

Browning Automatic Rifle (BAR) © 2006 Jupiterimages Corporation.

Also:

Many thanks to the staff of the Berman Museum of World History, in Anniston, Alabama, Cheryl Bragg, Executive Director; Dan Spaulding, Curator of Collections; Matt Mumbauer, Registrar; Adam Cleveland, Facilities Manager; Teresa Bradshaw, Office Manager; and especially Robert Lindley, Collections Manager, who proved an invaluable resource. Additional thanks to Tim Moon, Registrar of the Anniston Museum.